Women

IN RACING

In Their Own Words

John & Julia McEvoy

ECLIPSE PRESS

Lexington, Kentucky

Library of Congress Card Number: 2001086643

ISBN 1-58150-067-X

Printed in The United States
First Edition: September 2001

a division of The Blood-Horse, Inc.
PUBLISHERS SINCE 1916

CONTENTS

CONTENTS

Continued

A ny time there is a concentration of attention on one segment of society, the temptation to generalize, or draw sweeping conclusions, usually comes galloping up alongside.

That won't happen here, for that was never the point of this project — even though the book is entirely about contemporary women whose lives are devoted in some form or another to the Thoroughbred racehorse.

Instead, the purpose is to introduce to the reader a group of horse racing participants that is as varied and vital as it is interesting. It is made up of a cross-section of women from many parts of the United States, as well as England and Mexico.

Women currently occupy a wide variety of extremely significant roles in racing. Their presence and influence are apparent in every aspect of the sport, which is remarkable when one recalls that hardly more than a generation ago racing was still — as it had been for centuries — almost completely dominated by men. Where did these women come from? What prompted them to penetrate this male bastion and seek such vocations as jockey, trainer, owner-breeder, television commentator, veterinarian, photographer, track official, clocker, chart caller, pari-mutuel clerk, and groom?

The answers follow — provided by eighteen individuals whose backgrounds range all over the socio-economic spectrum, from the landed gentry to former migrant worker, with a rich layer of twenty-first century Americana in between.

Almost all of the women were driven by a shared passion: a love of horses and Thoroughbred racing. Many of them were willing to make great personal sacrifices to stay in the sport. Some went places where few women had gone before, thus breaking new ground on journeys that were sometimes grueling, and often inspiring.

Their stories are recounted in their own words, and these words reflect determination, self-awareness, courage, humor, and a deep appreciation of the Thoroughbred horse and the life that swirls about it — year, after year, after year.

We consider it a privilege that these women agreed to share these stories with us. We are grateful to all of them.

We dedicate this book to all who work with and admire
the Thoroughbred horse, and to our families.

John and Julia McEvoy
Evanston, Illinois, 2001

C H A P T E R (1)

L I N D A   R I C E

ℕot Afraid of Hard Work

Oₙₑ of America's best young trainers was about to conclude another busy morning at rain-drenched Saratoga. With a thirty-horse stable split between two barns at the ancient Spa, logistical nightmares had to be addressed in addition to the soggy conditions that had resulted from some twelve straight hours of August rain.

But despite the weather, Linda Rice was in an excellent mood. Two nights earlier, at the final session of the Saratoga yearling sale, one of her clients, Harry Quadrucci, had bought three well-bred youngsters for a total of nearly $600,000.

This was a major development for Rice, who rarely had her talented hands on blue-blooded racing stock. Practicing her craft on much more modestly pedigreed runners, Rice — who was born in 1964 and who saddled her first winner in 1988 — has nevertheless saddled 332 winners and has had total earnings of more than $10.7 million through late May 2001. She has trained ten stakes winners, including graded-stakes win-

*ners Double Booked, Ready Jet Go, and Tenski. (When the last-
named captured the Queen Elizabeth II Challenge Cup in 1998, Rice
became the first woman trainer to win a grade I race at Keeneland.)*

*Notable among Rice's stakes winners in 2000 was City Zip, a nine-
thousand-dollar yearling she developed into the winner of the Sanford,
Saratoga Special, and Hopeful Stakes at Saratoga. Runner-up to City
Zip in the Sanford and finishing in a dead heat with him for the win in
the grade I Hopeful was Yonaguska, a $1.9-million yearling trained by
Hall of Famer D. Wayne Lukas, a longtime family friend. City Zip was
a finalist for champion two-year-old male in 2000.*

My family was from Wisconsin, and up there where we
lived people do a lot with horses — 4-H, horse shows,
rodeos; a lot of activities. They have fairs where they
race horses. My grandfather, Loyal Rice, drove logging horses. He
was a schoolteacher. He also showed Arabian horses and Quarter
Horses, and he raced some Arabians. He was born in Wisconsin,
with an Irish-German background.

Like his father, my dad (Clyde Rice) became a schoolteacher. He
taught science, and he coached wrestling. To supplement his
income from teaching, he started working with horses. He started
buying unbroke horses. He would work with them every day after
school, breaking them and training them, then reselling them for a
profit as saddle horses. He was, like, doing early pinhooking.

My dad grew up with Wayne Lukas, who is also from Antigo.

Her genuine affection
for horses has helped
Linda Rice succeed
as a trainer.

Wayne was a teacher and a coach (basketball), too. My dad and Wayne rodeoed together and bought horses together. They'd buy a bunch of wild, unbroke horses for seven-hundred dollars and then sell each of them, once they'd worked with them, for maybe five-hundred dollars. They could both teach young horses and young children. They were good at it.

Wayne and my dad worked their way through saddle horses to show horses to eventually racing some horses; first at fairs in Wisconsin, later in other places. My father is a very ambitious man. And, of course, that ambition carried down to his children.

En route to the winner's circle with City Zip.

Eventually this passion for the horses and the income from it was greater than his income from teaching. During the summers when I was maybe three or four years old, we'd go up to Canada, to Winnipeg, where he'd race horses until school started again. We (her parents and her brothers, Bryan, Curt, and Wayne) lived in a little twenty-foot trailer, camping out for the summer. They were good times. Oh, yeah, they were wonderful times.

After about two summers of that, my dad decided to give up school teaching. He moved the whole family to West Virginia. He sold our farm in Wisconsin. He had decided to race Thoroughbreds full time, and he used the money from the farm for horses. We found ourselves at Waterford Park, living in tack rooms for about a month until my dad got a trailer rented in a trailer park across the street from the racetrack. The grandparents, all our cousins, were back in Wisconsin. My grandmother, her name was Louise, would send "care packages" to us, stuff us kids liked, bubble gum and candy.

I was about six years old when we made that move. When Grandma sent stuff, I'd send her a letter back. One of the letters that I sent said, "We're having fun here at Waterford Park, and thank you for the stuff. We miss you." On the bottom, there was a P.S. that said, "Ms. Josh is in the sixth race on Friday." When my grandmother passed away ten years ago, my mother was going through things of hers and found that letter.

Anyway, my dad bought a few horses and then turned them into more horses. He is brilliant at making something out of nothing.

He went there with nothing, and he created something. We stayed there at Waterford for probably three years. Then my father decided to move to another racetrack, Penn National, which was just being opened up. He wanted to move forward to what he thought would be a better track. And he and my mother thought that area would be a better place to raise a family.

They put a down payment on a farm in Pennsylvania. This was a big move for them. I think they put down ten percent on a $75,000 farm. My brother Brian, he was the oldest child, remembers that my parents were standing in the yard looking at this farmhouse, and one of us kids said, "God, wouldn't it be wonderful to live here?" My parents didn't think they could afford to buy it. But with all the excitement from the kids, they just decided they were going to go ahead and do it.

My dad had to save his cash for the horses, so we lived in that farmhouse with no furniture for about a year. It was an old house with a log-cabin kitchen. We slept on the floor in sleeping bags. But we had our own bedrooms. That was very exciting for us. Our stuff was in boxes. One of the boxes had an old black-and-white television set on it. When I look back on what my family went through, it's amazing to me.

It was a struggle at first, but we had a great time as a family. We loved living there. This was a farm on which they had raised cows. My dad renovated the cow barns into horse barns. He built ten stalls at first, then another ten, and just kept on expanding. He got the horse business going just like he did at Waterford Park. And eventually my father was leading trainer at Penn National. He's a very ambitious person and a terrific trainer.

It was when we were living in that house that I first got a real grip on the fact that horses and racing weren't just my family's interest, but that it was, like, a world issue. When I was nine, that was 1973, we all watched Secretariat when he won the Kentucky Derby. We were all watching it on this little black-and-white TV up on a cardboard box in the living room.

That was my first memory of the excitement of horse racing. I mean, my father had raced and trained a zillion horses in Canada, West Virginia, but I never really had grasped before that, wow, this is a big deal, an attraction. With Secretariat being all over the newspapers and in the magazines, it dawned on me, "this is more than I thought it was."

I was pretty involved with the horses. All of us were. All my brothers became jockeys and rode until they got too heavy. *(Editors' note: Curt Rice led the nation's apprentices in 1979 with 312 wins.)* When we'd come home from school, my brother Curt and I would take care of twenty horses in the barn — my dad and the older boys were taking care of forty at the racetrack. It would take us about an hour and a half. But it would take a lot longer if we fought about who was going to do what (laughs). As I got older, I decided the quickest way to get the work done was to do the jobs Curt didn't want to do.

1 RICE

We lived so far out in the country, twenty miles from school, we didn't have friends to be with after school. My parents would let us be involved in sports. My brothers wrestled — Bryan won two state championships and Wayne was 23-0 in his senior year. They were gymnasts, too, and so was I. Because I was a gymnast, they were trying to recruit me to be a cheerleader. And I wanted to be a cheerleader. This was a big point for me, because my father said, "If we are going to travel that far to take you to school, you're going to be playing a sport, not cheering for it." And that was that.

I was disappointed. But we gained so much, too. We gained the work ethic. But it was hard. When I was sixteen, my oldest brother, Bryan, was gone to Tampa, and Wayne and Curt were riding races; they were never home. I just felt kind of isolated, and I went through a terrible depression. I used to go home from school, and I'd do my chores, and I'd go to my bedroom and wouldn't leave. My mother took me to doctors; she was very concerned. I couldn't seem to help myself. Then my folks packed me off to Florida with my youngest brother, Curt, and the depression was gone.

I had a pretty strong fear of horses until I was about twelve, maybe fourteen — a fear of riding them I mean, not working with them. When I was a young child in Wisconsin, I was injured on a horse. He got loose with me and ran around and scared me. After that I had a fear that my parents had to struggle with. My father was trying to buy horses that I could ride. I had a bunch of rotten little ponies. You know they can terrorize you. We bought pony after pony. We never got the right one. I just didn't get over that fear for a long time, even though my family's whole life was involved with horses.

As I got older, this fear I had was a problem. It became a bit of a family problem and an issue. Nobody else was afraid of riding horses, but I was afraid. My dad would force me to ride, and it was very tense for me and difficult. So that was a struggle for me at that age.

Finally, I got free of it. I was about fourteen. I started riding Thoroughbreds, and all of a sudden — it was like a light-bulb effect — I understood how to make them do what I wanted them to do. There was a friend, Candy Little, a girl who worked for my father, she was really good with animals, and she showed me a few things. And all of a sudden, it just came together. I understood what made them tick. I got over my fear. I knew how to communicate with them. And then I started breaking horses and later galloping horses at the racetrack.

When the light bulb finally went off for me, it was connected to one particular horse — a very, very difficult horse named Family Style. Now, she went on to be the two-year-old filly champion of 1985 for Wayne Lukas. He bought her in a package deal from my father. But she was almost impossible in the early days.

I broke her for my father. I'd gallop her around out in the field and try to teach her commands, and she would cry out like a baby. It was just the strangest thing. Before we ride them, we get them used to the equipment and the directions — stop, start, turn, you know. Family Style would try to crawl underneath a gate to get in with another horse because she was so scared. And she would just whine — hoo, hoo, hoo — like a child. But with attention and kindness, that helped her through her mental struggle, her fears. She ended up being a champion. I learned from her, and she learned from me. We helped one another.

I remember Wayne coming to Penn National and being up in the clockers' stand with my father, and I would be galloping horses. Wayne said to my father, "If your daughter ever wants a job with me in New York, she's welcome."

I couldn't help but thinking about that after City Zip beat Wayne's colt Yonaguska (in the Sanford). Wayne was very gracious after the race. He grabbed my hand warmly and congratulated me. It's kind of a strange phenomenon — Wayne kind of treats me as if I'm his daughter.

When I started at the track for my father in the summers, I was rubbing horses. Then I started galloping a few. Next thing you know, I was getting better and better, and then I was galloping eight and rubbing four. I remember my father was real proud of me because I'm sixteen or seventeen, and I've become his best exercise rider — my brothers were all gone and riding races by then — and his best groom. There was a filly named Dream Harder. I loved to gallop her, and I groomed her, and she looked magnificent in the afternoon when she'd race. It was very rewarding. My father was proud of me. He'd tell me, "Boy, you've done a nice job with that one."

My brothers and I all owned horses. I was about nine when I got my first one from my father. I used the seventy-two dollars I had in my piggy bank to buy my piece of my first horse. And I was in the red until I was fifteen. That year my father and I claimed a horse named Money Saver for $6,500. We each owned half. Money Saver finished second three times in a row. My brother Curt is seventeen; he's riding the horse. Then we dropped Money Saver back in for $6,500. He wins by a neck, and he gets claimed. I had never seen Curt happier than when he won that race. I hated to part with Money Saver, but when you make money on a horse you can learn to part with it. I learned that early.

After training in Pennsylvania, my father made a whole new business of buying young horses and developing them and selling them to Wayne Lukas. Family Style was one. Tiltalating was another that Wayne bought and brought to New York. She won the Sorority and the Spinaway (both in 1984). I learned a lot about young horses from watching my father and Wayne.

With Bryan off in Tampa with horses for my father, and Curt riding races, that left me in the position of assisting my father. I was young, but the stable employees accepted me because I worked so hard. You never make an enemy of somebody if you're doing more work than they are. I wasn't the guy standing at the end of the shed row telling them what to do. I was doing more than anybody else myself.

When I was ten years old, I met David Applebee. His mother

worked for a trainer that my father knew. David and I were in the same grade. When we were both sixteen, we were both galloping horses at the racetrack. David wanted to be a jockey. He got his apprentice license, and he did quite well.

That's about when we started dating. I remember he had asked me out for about two months nonstop. He drove out to my parents' house to pick me up, and he was dressed in a sports jacket and a tie. His car is washed and everything. I didn't want to go out with him that night. I told my brother Curt to go out to the car and tell David I was sick.

My father had a fit. After David drove away, my father grounded me. He said that what I'd done was horrible, that I should never treat anybody like that again. He was very upset. So, I eventually wind up marrying David. My parents weren't too happy about that, either. What bothered them was that he had gotten mixed up with drugs and alcohol. He wasn't a straight arrow any longer. I knew he'd been into all that bad stuff, but he was fine then, and I was in love with him.

He went to Cleveland to ride races. I went to college for my second year (Penn State), but I wasn't very happy. I was always going home, going back and forth with the horses. When he came to college with an engagement ring, I didn't need a lot of persuading. I went home for Christmas, we got engaged — it was a Sunday, my dad's fiftieth birthday — then I quit school. We got married nine months later. He was the one for me — had been since I was sixteen. I was twenty-three. But after a while his habits with drugs and alcohol were really weighing on me. The marriage lasted about three years.

My folks moved from Pennsylvania to Florida. My dad bought a farm there and set up a breaking and pinhooking business. I went down there to help break horses. There was this lot of fillies that hadn't been broken, and I picked out one, a great big filly with a white face. She didn't have a name. My dad didn't even own her. But he bought her then.

This was Ready Jet Go. I broke and trained her, and she was a strange bird. You couldn't intimidate her. She wouldn't respond to anything. I thought she might be blind, and maybe deaf and dumb too. I'd be out in the field, and I'd be so angry with her. But she just had this real tough personality. I finally got through to her.

This was when I was still married, so my husband and I take six horses up to Garden State. He's riding them; I'm training them — four of my dad's horses, two for clients. This was a big deal, us going up there. I don't think I would ever have gone off on my own without my husband. I probably just would have remained in the family business on the farm.

I was scared, nervous. I'm galloping three of the six horses and rubbing three; my husband's rubbing the others. We've got Ready Jet Go with us. She wins three races in a row, the third one a stakes at Pimlico, the [1988] Flirtation with my husband riding her.

This is great, right? We were in love. We were happy. David's doing great. But then he fell off the trail with alcohol and then drugs. The next thing you know, we're fighting and he's gone.

I'm in New Jersey now with six horses by myself. I refused to go home. I was hurt, but my pride wouldn't let me. I was going to tough it out. Also, I didn't want to hear that my parents had said to me, "Don't marry him...don't marry him."

The meet closed at Garden State, so I moved my trailer across the river to Philadelphia Park. I was still trying to work it out with my husband. But I drove to Penn National one night, and he was living with this other girl that he had lived with before our marriage, and that was it. I drove one hundred miles an hour back to Philadelphia in the pouring rain. I was crushed. I started going to a psychologist, who helped me a lot, and after a while, you know, I got my head clear. The next year I went to Monmouth Park with nine horses; then I got up to thirteen. I'm galloping eleven myself in order to save money; I'm doing everything around the barn.

A friend of mine worked in the racing secretary's office there. One day he said some guy from Michigan had called him looking for a trainer. My friend recommended me. "She'll work really hard," he told him.

Next thing you know, I get these two horses from Michigan. One's supposedly a stakes horse — some little dink Michigan-bred race that he'd run third in — and one's a claiming horse. When they get off the trailer, I'm thinking, "This has got to be the stakes horse." Nope. The ugly horse was the stakes horse. It was Double

Booked. I had no idea he'd ever turn into a stakes horse. *(Editors'*
note: Under Rice's direction, Double Booked won ten stakes and
some $800,000.)

I run Double Booked for twenty ($20,000 claiming) on the dirt,
and he runs fifth. We run him for eighteen, and he runs second. I
was galloping him, and he was very tough to gallop. So was Ready
Jet Go — she pulled me so bad one morning that my back went out.
I called my buddy in the secretary's office asking if he knew a chi-
ropractor. I wanted to get an appointment for after that afternoon's
races. Double Booked is in that day. I'm lying on the feed sacks in
the feed room because they're cold on my back, trying to get ready
to go to the paddock. When I saddle Double Booked, my back
popped, and I passed out from the pain. So the ambulance comes.
I'm in the paddock lying in the grass, and the horses go on the
track, and Double Booked runs second, gets beat a nose. It was the
last time he ever ran on the dirt.

I was in the hospital for a few days, and they said, "Well, you've
got a broken back." It was an old fracture that was aggravated.
This friend called my parents. I've got these horses to train, and I'm
in the hospital. My father flew up, got on the last flight, and
showed up at the hospital at one o'clock in the morning. He stayed
until I got out of the hospital.

I'd been in the hospital before. One year, when we were breaking horses, I was injured pretty badly. I'd gotten thrown from a
horse and that night I had internal bleeding. My parents took me

to the hospital. They cut me open this way. They cut me open that way. It was internal bleeding, and they couldn't find where it was. I about died; I was just a few minutes from being in the box.

Ready Jet Go, she was an amazing, talented horse; she kept winning stakes. So I decided to take her to Saratoga. First horse I ever raced there. It was a big deal. I drove her up there myself — not in a horse van, but in my dad's cattle trailer.

I remember saying to my dad, "How am I going to get her in the trailer at Philadelphia Park?" I take feed sacks out of the feed room and build a ramp and put rubber mats in the trailer so I can jump her up into there. And she does it fine.

When I get to Saratoga, when I pulled up in the cattle trailer, well they were kind of amazed. They were shocked, let me tell you. We put Ready Jet Go in the receiving barn; that's where she stayed. I stayed in that little motel there right on the corner of Nelson Avenue.

She wasn't nominated to the Test, which is for three-year-old fillies, so we put her in the Ballerina Stakes against older mares. She runs third, only gets beat this far. After the race I'm getting ready to leave, to drive back to Pennsylvania. Bloodstock agents follow me back to the barn. And there were some reporters wanting to interview me about this filly.

I don't want them to see me putting her back in the cattle trailer. I can't say, "Gentlemen, would you mind looking the other way for a minute?" A friend of mine was there, and I told him, "I'm going to pull the truck down the road there in that grassy area and then back it up." I do that, and it's good; it's kind of downhill.

Now, this time, I've got no feed sacks or rubber mats to help me get the filly back in the trailer. This is hilarious. I'm thinking, "Won't this be a sight for all these people following me? How am I going to do this?"

Remember, this is the filly that when I was out in the field with her that day I thought was blind, deaf, and dumb. So, I pick up one front foot, and I'm thinking, "Oh, this is ridiculous," and she immediately just jumps up into the trailer. She bailed me right out. It was amazing. And all those people were still there and watching as I drove off with her in the cattle trailer. That was my introduction to Saratoga.

That fall Ready Jet Go won the Meadowlands Budweiser Breeders' Cup going six furlongs. She goes in 1:08 2/5 and ties the track record. It was a $150,000 race. Now, this is my biggest win ever. So my father and I take her to the Breeders' Cup. She's a brilliant sprinter. And what happened was that she didn't pick up a foot that day in the Sprint at Churchill Downs because of our inexperience.

My father put up $20,000 to supplement her. We put her on Lasix (a medication that controls exercise-induced pulmonary hemorrhage) for the first time. A lot of the European horses that came over ran on Lasix for the first time. It was a big mistake for us, though. We almost had to drag her to the paddock. The effect Lasix had on her was to tranquilize her. She broke last and finished last.

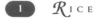

That was our first trip to the Breeders' Cup. *(Editors' note: With Ready Jet Go in 1988, Rice became the first female trainer to saddle a Breeders' Cup Day starter. In November of 2000, Rice returned to the Breeders' Cup at Churchill Downs, finishing seventh in the Juvenile with City Zip.)*

I think the reason more women don't have the so-called "big horses" is lack of opportunity. It really makes no difference what sex you are talent-wise. Men and women both have the same capabilities to train horses and get the same results. But in order to get to the top of the game, a woman has to work twice as hard because she's not offered the same opportunities.

The hard-work part doesn't bother me. My family worked twice as hard because we were broke. It was a happy broke, but it was broke. But we were taught to work long and hard, to go that extra yard, and it'll come back to you in tenfold. It did to my father. So, my working extra hard wasn't because I was a woman in a man's world. That was the way I was raised. I think that my odds of succeeding as a woman in this man-oriented business were better than for other women because I had this tremendous work ethic from a young age. That pushed me in the right direction. And despite the odds, I was able to continue and succeed and move forward.

What makes all the work worthwhile is I just love to train good horses, and I like the self-satisfaction of creating a good horse, one that can succeed. When I first started training and had a little success, people said, "Well, her father sends her all those horses; she's got it easy." In their minds any success I had was due to my father.

Well, frankly, I was training my father's horses initially. But then I got one or two clients from him, and then I got some of my own, and it grew. And after awhile, they couldn't say that it was all of my father's doing. They'd seen me out there working seven days a week, year after year after year. Finally, they no longer felt like what success I was having I had gotten undeservedly.

When I trained Ready Jet Go and Double Booked, well, I was proving to myself that I deserved good opportunities, that my hard work could produce something. But it's probably only in the last five years that I've gotten to the point where I feel like I'm pretty capable of doing this job. There are guys who are presented more opportunities than I am. Maybe it's my sex; maybe it's my background. Maybe if I'd come from a different background, been born and raised in Kentucky, or if I'd been an assistant to somebody like Charlie Whittingham or Wayne Lukas, maybe then I'd be given more opportunities. I mean, I see a lot more women assistant trainers now. But you still don't see that many women training big stables for the big owners.

When I see Jenine Sahadi, who has won two Breeders' Cup races, and I read that she is struggling to have people hire her, that is demoralizing. It really is. I told my father once, "I go to these Miami sales, and it seems like every good horse that is being purchased is sent to the same guys to train. I'm down there fighting this battle to purchase good horses, and I'm getting outbid, and the same trainers are getting all the good horses. Even the good buy-backs are going to the same guys! A lot of them are my age."

I remember calling my dad from my cell phone in the parking lot outside the sales pavilion in Miami. I'm in total frustration. I tell him, "Everything good that's bought goes to these guys."

My father puts it all in perspective. He tells me, "Don't get down in the mouth. We'll figure it out. We'll get it going in the right direction."

There's no question, I got a lot of great things from my dad, and there are things he excels at that I don't. He's great at breaking and training young horses. And he goes to auctions around the country and buys some magnificent Quarter Horses and Appaloosas. Then he'll teach them tricks. He'll teach them to bow and to lie down on command. He does all these things, just like the *Horse Whisperer*. That's not my strength.

My strength is in taking these young horses to the races. My mother said the funniest thing once when my dad was telling me how to do something with one of my horses. She said, "Clyde, when you were thirty-six, did you think that you needed anybody's help in figuring out what to do with horses? Well, your daughter doesn't either. She's got twice as much experience as you had at her age."

I think I'm probably a lot easier on horses than my father was. For instance, if a horse wasn't performing, my dad might have thought that it didn't want to perform. When I'm training a horse and it does-n't perform, I find it's because it's not capable of performing.

I'm not a big believer in jockeys using the stick (whip). Horses run as much as they can. If they're too sore to try, you shouldn't be running them. And you have to help them with the mental stress and pressure of racing by showing them things — schooling them in the paddock and at the gate — so that their heart isn't ready to jump out of their chest when they get over there.

City Zip, well, we didn't have much time up here before his first Saratoga start in the Sanford. But he has a terrific mind. I'd take him into the paddock between races, and he is just the coolest; you know, he's just a pro. When I've taken him to the paddock at Belmont before races, it was like I got no reaction from him. No emotion, no nothing. It was almost like he didn't care, which I wasn't too crazy about. But he ran well anyway.

Anyway, when I took City Zip to the paddock here (at Saratoga), he's maybe a smidgen nervous about it. He walks into his stall, and he takes two deep breaths. He did it real quiet   I mean if you weren't looking you would never know he was doing it. He's only two, but he's smart. He's a pro.

You have to have a passion for the horse itself in order to have success with them. I happen to like horses, all of them. They still amaze me how smart they are. Some I like more than others, but I like them all. And the ones that become stars, you just love them more.

At this stage I take delight in the fact that now I'm a homeowner in New York and I have a successful business. I'm recognized as a New York trainer. I think people realize that I can select horses to race and train them to win. I'm getting more support from my owners at the sales.

What do I look for in a horse? Well, a lot of times it's a matter of economics. My father and Wayne Lukas buy the same way. They buy an athlete and then depending on what their budget is, that tells you how much pedigree they can have with it.

The horse has to have good motion. A key thing for me is that he has to have a long shoulder. The shoulder is much more important than the hip. A long shoulder will support a lot of different hips on horses. It took me years to learn that part of it. I like a good, straight hind leg, and I like them to have width at the hock.

Again, most important is going to be their motion. They have to have a good rhythm to their walk, like a good athlete. It's like watching a basketball player. I go to the [New York] Knicks games. Latrell Sprewell, he looks to me like the best athlete. It doesn't matter if it's people or horses, if you watch enough of them you're going to be able to recognize the best athletes.

It took me years to understand that when I had a horse that wasn't doing well it wasn't necessarily because of me. For years, when a horse didn't succeed I thought it must be because of something I was doing wrong. But I learned that wasn't necessarily the case. They weren't succeeding because they weren't very good. They couldn't run. Once I got that figured out, well, that was very important. I got to the point where I knew that some could run and some can't, and don't beat yourself up over it.

I've had women ask me, women who are trainers or who want to be trainers, "How did you do it?" The main thing I tell them, "You have to get yourself financially stable." My father told me that years ago. "Then," he said, "you can make good decisions about how much pressure to put on horses."

What he means by that is that you don't have to cash a bet on a horse in order to survive. You don't have to do things you shouldn't be doing in order to pay the feed man. If it's raining for two weeks, I don't breeze my horses for two weeks because I don't have to have them ready for a race in order to pay the feed man or pay my rent. If the horses don't earn money for months, you have to be able to get through a tough period like that and not change what you are doing.

When I first came to New York, it was on December 7 of 1991. I remember sitting in a Dunkin' Donuts waiting for my horses to arrive from the Meadowlands. I was nervous and scared. It wasn't easy at first, making a move like this. I struggled for the next four or five years before things really started going the right way.

Like I told the women who asked me the question, in order to be financially secure I reduced the overhead. I did the work myself. I didn't pay to have an exercise rider or an assistant trainer. I groomed the horses and washed the buckets myself. I lived in a basement apartment. I just recently bought the house — the same one that had the basement apartment I lived in for six years. I'd been trying to move up for years, and I finally did. Compared to where I was when I started, well, like my father, I created something out of nothing.

I'd eventually like to be married and have a family. When I'm forty, at that point I'm going to re-evaluate where I'm at. Frankly, I might decide to have children, and I need to be freed up from training for a while in order to do that.

If that happens, I want to be at a point in my career where I've proved to myself and to the racing industry that I'm capable of doing this job as a trainer. I don't want marriage and a family to sabotage me completely in my career. I want to be able later to come back to training if that's what I decide to do.

There were two main things my father told me when I started out. One was what I said before about being financially secure. The other thing he said was that he had never known "a successful female trainer who was successfully married."

And so I said to him, "Well, I'm just going to have to be the first."

P A T T I (B A R T O N) B R O W N E
& D O N N A B A R T O N B R O T H E R S

$\mathcal{P}$ioneering Spirits

Between them they rode the winners of 2,333 races. But the mother-daughter combination of Patti (Barton) Browne and Donna Barton Brothers, their careers separated in years by only a generation, worked in dramatically different eras for women jockeys in Thoroughbred racing.

Patti was an orphan, born in 1944, then adopted and raised in Florida. After graduating from high school, and over the objections of her parents, she abruptly left home to join a rodeo. She married a fellow rodeo performer, Charlie Barton, and had three children with him: Leah, born in 1964; Donna, 1966; and Jerry, 1967. Patti and Charlie divorced shortly after Jerry's birth, leaving Patti as the sole support of this young family.

She was able to do so best as a jockey: Patti was one of the first half-dozen women licensed as a jockey. (Barbara Jo Rubin on February 22, 1969, at Charles Town became the first to win a race at *a pari-mutuel track.) Like other pioneer women riders in what was a male-dominated profession, her path hit potholes of gender prejudice, discrimination, and professional jealousy, particularly after her riding prowess became obvious. But a combination of brashness, savvy, strength, and talent carried her through. Her sense of humor didn't hurt, either. As she noted more than once, her definition of "penis envy" was a "cold winter night at Waterford Park (in West Virginia) when you have to go to the bathroom and you're wearing layers of clothes. That's the only time I had penis envy."*

Patti won her first race and 178 more in 1969 at a recognized track, old Pikes Peak Meadows, in Colorado. That year she set a single-season record for a woman. She subsequently made Waterford Park her base. A personal career highlight for this former rodeo rider/cocktail waitress/exercise girl/single mother was winning a race at Keeneland. Another occurred on Mother's Day of 1983 when Patti beat both daughter Leah and son Jerry in a race at old Centennial Park in Denver. When she retired in 1984 after suffering severe injuries in a spill at Fairmount Park in southern Illinois, Patti ranked as the world's leading female rider with 1,202 victories.

After her divorce from Charlie Barton, Patti married three more times. Her most recent marriage was to trainer Jack Browne, who died in 1992. Today Patti makes her home in northwest Kentucky with Leah and Leah's four children — "I'm a live-in grandma," she said.

Donna was born in New Mexico. She began galloping horses as a

Donna Barton Brothers
did not intend to follow
in the bootsteps of her
mother, Patti Browne.

teenager, motivated at first by a desire to earn money for college. But once she learned she "just loved to ride," she set her sights on being a jockey. Donna began riding professionally in 1987 and notched her first win at Birmingham Park.

She has a deep appreciation of the challenges her mother faced breaking in as a jockey at the end of the turbulent sixties. "I thank God it was her that had to do it first and not me," Donna said.

When Donna retired in September of 1998 at the age of thirty-two, less than a month prior to her marriage to trainer Frank Brothers, she had won 1,131 races. She earned many of those victories over the kind of high-class competition that her mother only dreamed of.

She holds the Churchill Downs record for most stakes wins by a female jockey and rode numerous winners for Hall of Fame trainer D. Wayne Lukas. It was Lukas who gave her the mount on Hennessy, whom Donna guided to a second-place finish in the 1995 Breeders' Cup Juvenile.

In 1999, Donna signed on as a racing analyst for Churchill Downs and Fair Grounds. She made her national network debut as an interviewer in the course of NBC's television coverage of the 2000 Breeders' Cup at Churchill — on horseback, of course. She also was part of the network's 2001 Kentucky Derby coverage.

Patti: When this thing came about where women were starting to ride, I was in New Mexico. And at that time, in 1968, they would let women have a groom's license, trainer license, and pony license. But they wouldn't let them have an exercise license.

Well, I was doing a little galloping illegally in the early fall of sixty-eight. So then by later in sixty-eight, Kathy Kusner had won her case. *(Editors' note: Kusner was denied a license by the Maryland Racing Commission in 1967. She successfully appealed in the courts and became the first licensed female jockey.)*

That gave me the go-ahead to take out an exercise license, and they had to give it to me. Okay, now I'm galloping horses for a dollar a head. And you know what kind of horses I'm getting — not very nice ones. And I would have horses that I'd go on the track at the three-quarters chute (an extension of the backstretch) and

Brothers and Hennessy, a colt who nearly won the Breeders' Cup Juvenile.

they'd rear up and fall over backwards. And within thirty minutes that same thing would be said in the kitchen again: "That girl fell off again."

I'm doing this for a dollar a head. I said, "This is ridiculous; I'm going to kill myself for a damn dollar." And I was tending bar (at night) for a dollar an hour. So when the women were just starting out riding, I thought why shouldn't I give it a try? If you want to do something and you set your mind to it, you can do anything you want to do.

Donna: I'll tell you, much to my mother's credit, I don't know where she got her strong determination from, because she didn't grow up with a mother or dad telling her, "Sure, honey, you can do whatever you think you can do." They were always, "No, you're not going to do that."

Patti: It must be in the genes.

Donna: I remember growing up as a kid and telling my mom all the time: "You know, Mom, you don't have to worry about living in a nursing home, because I'm going to be a millionaire and I'm going to take care of you." And she'd always be like, "Yeah, that's nice, sweetie." And then one day, I was about fourteen, and she and I are sitting at the table in the dining room. I think I was doing my homework or something and she was getting dinner ready. It hit me: Is that just a dream or can I do whatever? Yeah, I'm going to be a millionaire — right! And I said, "Mom, you know how I always tell you that I'm going to be a millionaire and take care of you?" And she said, "Yes." And I said, "Do you think that's just a dream that kids have or do you really think I am going to be a millionaire? Because I think I am." She said, "I think you can do anything you think you can do." And I said, "All right! That's settled." (Donna and Patti look at each other and burst out laughing.)

Patti: I always tried to do the best I could at the best possible racetracks I could do it at. But there was one other job that was even more important. I had these children, and they had to be in a place where they could go to school year round. So that's why my career was West Virginia, Pennsylvania, Ohio, kind of — you know — not too high up.

So I'd go out and work at the track mornings and come home and have the afternoon to shop, or go to the doctor's office or school, or take a nap. I was there when the kids came home from school, and I got dinner started. I'd put dinner on the table and then

Patti Browne's most meaningful victory: a claiming race at Keeneland.

leave for the jockeys' room. I always had someone there, a babysitter. I never sat down to eat.

I can remember times at Waterford. I'm riding three races, early and late, so I've got this time. I would bring my portable sewing machine to the jocks' room. And I said, "I'm tired of riding with all of you raggedy-ass jockeys." Because their pants would get all torn up. So they'd bring them down and I'd fix them. I didn't charge; it was just something to do so I wouldn't have to ride with these raggedy-ass jockeys. I fixed their pants.

I couldn't stand day racing. When you're a single parent, there's too many things that you have to handle, like the school, the doctor…You can't do day racing. Night racing is okay. It's like working a split shift. Racetrack in the morning to gallop horses for everybody, and by doing this you get the mounts.

It wasn't a matter of the competition, or the bucks. I was doing the best I could at the best possible level that I could.

Donna: That's why I always had wings. Because I knew what Mom had given up to stay in one place to raise the children the best she could and make a good living. So whenever I'd get to a place where I'd [think], "Well, I'm doing fine here, but there is that chance to go over there [to another track]. But then I'd have to start over again."

But then I'd say, "Hey, there's nothing holding me here. I don't have three kids to support, a husband to answer to. I have the freedom and I will use it."

Patti: The levels that Donna achieved in racing were far superior to where I rode.

Donna: But not any easier.

Patti: You know, it's the same ballgame but it's a different ballgame.

Donna: When I started, she had paved the way. [Jockey] Patty Cooksey likes to say she didn't blaze the trail, but she made it a little smoother for the ones who followed. I came into the game at a very late stage. It's tough to be a jockey, but it's tough for Joe and Ed *and* Jane. It's a really tough occupation. But I was always thankful for what Mom had done before me, because she had to get into physical altercations in the jocks' room. There were girls, Kathy Kusner, who had to go to court just to be able to ride. I wouldn't have done that. I absolutely wouldn't have done that, because it didn't mean that much to me. I didn't have kids to support and all that. I was going to ride, but, "Hey, don't make it a freakin' legal battle or anything!"

I remember a couple times when I first started where I wondered, "Man, am I going to have to fight with these guys, like my mom did?" There were a couple of times when I was mad enough that I would have.

There was this clerk of scales up at Rockingham Park. After a race this one rider was screaming at me and using foul language. I had the apprenticeship at the time, and I just cussed right back at him. I said, "If you have a problem, call the stewards and we'll watch the film," but I cussed right back at him.

That clerk of scales pulled me aside later and said, "I will not let them speak to the girl jocks that way. But I cannot prevent it if you're talking to them in the same way." And I said, "Gotcha! Hey, if you're going to intervene, then I'm out!" And I learned that the one thing I could always do was take the high road.

After that it was, "I'm really sorry that I bothered you, but if you would like to call the stewards, I'll watch the film with you tomorrow." Or, "I'm sorry I bothered you. I'll watch the replay with you, and you show me what I did wrong." But my mom didn't have that advantage.

Patti: No.

Donna: But what happened with her was some guy would be hitting her across the back with his whip!

(Editors' note: Donna's reference is to a race during which a male jockey intentionally struck Patti with his whip. Later, the two fought and were then confronted by the stewards. To prove what had happened to her, Patti pulled down her pants to reveal the welt on her buttocks.)

Patti: Okay, it was sad that I dropped my pants in front of the stewards. But the reality of it was Peb [*Daily Racing Form* cartoonist Pierre Bellocq] had drawn a cartoon about a month before this incident. And he showed a picture, it was a cartoon — there's a girl in a steward's office and the caption reads, "So you want to see where he hit me with the whip?" That was the comment. So there had been this jock who *did* hit me leaving the quarter pole. I mean hit me so soundly you could go in the jocks' room and see the imprint. He came back to the jocks' room. We got into it. So anyway the stewards came down to the jocks' room. And that's when I...

Donna: Wait, wait. He didn't just come down to the jocks' room. You were hiding around the corner, waiting for him to come down to the jocks' room, and you went after him!

Patti: Well, when the stewards came down, I said, you know last month Peb drew a cartoon to this effect, but, by God, I'll show you. Right there! (Patti points to the back of her right thigh.) I mean is that dropping your pants? I don't think it is. Donna thinks it is. Anyway, I showed them the popper mark. And then it really irritated this guy that he got fined seventy-five dollars and I got fined fifty dollars, and he wanted to know how come. Well, he had used a piece of equipment to hit me, so he got a seventy-five-dollar fine, I got a fifty-dollar fine.

There was another fight. It ended up they talked about it on the [Johnny] Carson Show. And what I said (Carson quoted her response to the stewards) was bleeped out in Boston. That was funny to me.

Fights in the jocks' room don't last any length of time. So I had a fight in the jocks' room, I don't remember what it was all about, but it ended up in a wrestling match. In the position I was in, there was only one thing I can grab (his testicles). And at that time, the fight is broken up. And they take him off into the jocks' room. And he hollers back: "Well, you can tell her that's the closest she's been to a man in a long time." I said, "You can tell him there was hardly anything to get hold of." And it's funny that that was bleeped in Boston, because it's really not anything. But it's the ultimate male put-down.

Donna: Women like my mom, Patty Cooksey, Sandy Schiffers, and Julie Krone, they showed that it's possible for a woman to be as talented as a man in this profession. And they had to just like go out there and lay all the groundwork and just demand attention and demand their rights and show that they could do it.

But by the time I came around, men, pretty much, in our game were of the frame of mind that, "Yeah, I've seen a girl rider make it once or twice, but you're going to have to show me, for me to believe you can do it." The respect was there, but you did have to earn it still. It wasn't just an automatic thing.

I think tensions in the jockey colony exist among males, too. I really don't think it's different. Like I think there are riders who want *not* to like Pat Day because of how well he does. But you can't help but to like the little guy. I mean he's just so damn likeable, and he's a good rider, and you have to respect him.

I'm sure there were plenty of people when they met me, given the fact that I was a girl, yeah, they didn't want to like me. But then they watch me ride. They see how hard I work, and they see that I'm a nice person, and they can't go, "I just don't like her." It was easier for me than it was for her.

And plus the male mentality was much different back when Mom started. Back when *she* started, if their wives didn't have dinner ready when they got home, they were pissed. So they can't imagine somebody letting their wife out of the house to come in here and take money out of their pocket.

When things got difficult I always had Leah to call, or Jerry to call, or my friends, or a boyfriend. Mom, who *did* you call? Was there ever anybody when you said, "Hey, I really need to talk to somebody right now."

(Patti shakes her head "no.")

Donna: Well, you poor little thing! (They laugh loudly.)

Patti: That's probably why I went through so many marriages in my life. That's why I tried so often. And I think the one thing that the men in my life could not accept was being *part* of my life. They thought that upon marriage, they would become my *whole* life. They were an important part of my life. But they were not my whole life. I was riding!

The thing about racing is: how many jobs can you have where you have the opportunity to be a winner? As a schoolteacher, you may finally get the point across to that kid and really feel like a winner. But horse racing is in front of God and all those people; it's more apparent.

Donna: I've gone through some pretty low times, but you just win one race — even if it's a $10,000-claiming race — it'll make all those other weeks worthwhile. It does do that.

Patti: The race that I'm fondest of having won was the one race I won at Keeneland. It was a $10,000-claiming race. At that level of racing it's a pretty low-level race. But I was prouder of that than the stakes races I'd won. *(Editors' note: To Patti, winning at the prestigious Kentucky racetrack, Keeneland, outshone any stakes she won at lower-level tracks.)* And then after Donna ends up fourth leading rider at Keeneland... (Patti grins broadly.)

Of my three kids, there was one who had no interest in horses or racing. (She nods in Donna's direction.) I was amazed when she decided to go work on the track and gallop. And she did very well; she had a real good job with Van Berg (Hall-of-Fame trainer Jack Van Berg). Being an exercise girl, she had a good job, made good money. But it's no direction to a life.

Race riding gives you a direction, okay? There are a lot of goals. With galloping, what do you do? Gallop a tougher horse? It just doesn't have the goals to it that race riding does. There are so many similarities between her career and mine, in a way. After she started, she really fell in love with it. Right? (She turns to Donna.)

Donna: Well, I had been galloping horses for four years, and somebody offered me some horses to train. I was twenty-one. I said, well, I've got to do something with my life; I can't be a gallop girl forever. So, okay, let me just ride a race first and eliminate that as a career choice, and then I'll train your horses.

Honestly, back then galloping horses and thinking about training, I really didn't see being a jockey as a challenge. (Patti snorts in laughter.) My mother was a jockey, for God's sake. What kind of a challenge is that? (Patti laughs even louder.) My mother, my brother, my sister...I mean jockey-schmockey, do something else with your life!

But I thought training horses would be more of a challenge. But then I got out there and rode my first race and I was like, "This is *not* that easy!"

I had been born and raised on the racetrack, so I didn't think I would be at all nervous. It was night racing; it was Birmingham. I galloped horses that morning, cleaned tack, went home, napped, and all morning everyone's like, "Are you nervous?" — "No, I'm not nervous." Well, I woke up from my nap running to the bathroom! Evidently my stomach was nervous. I wasn't, but my stomach was. I was like, "I *cannot* take off my *first* mount!" (Both mom and daughter laugh.)

Luckily my brother Jerry was there. He was a calming force. He had quit riding because he had gotten too big. And he was there with his camera taking pictures. And it's funny because I have the picture. I came back after that first race; I came in fifth. And I came back, and I just walked away [from the horse].

I don't take off my saddle or anything. (Patti laughs loudly.) I don't know where to go. I'm getting ready to take off my chin strap, and I'm saying, "That was *sooo* much fun! I can't believe I waited all this time! And it was *fast*. There was a *lot* going on!" I don't remember the details of the race, just that it was exciting, and it was what I wanted to do.

(Editors' note: Donna was so excited by the experience that she forgot it's part of the jockey's job to take the saddle off, carry it to the scale, and get weighed in after the race. Then the rider generally gives it to a valet. No jock ever just walks away and leaves the saddle on the horse — unless, of course, it's her first race!)

Patti: The one thing that people always bring up is: "You know, you had that terrible spill, and you think it's okay for her to ride?"

I never encouraged any of my kids to be riders at any time. Right? (Patti turns to Donna.)

Donna: She never discouraged us or encouraged us to be riding. But I do know that when I started riding, Mom was like, "Well, how'd you like it?" And I was like, "I loved it!" I could tell that she was so happy and excited and relieved.

Patti: Well, she had a *direction*! Okay?

Donna: The one thing Mom would always say when people would say, "Well, our daughter wants to become a jockey, what do you think?" The one thing she'd always say was, "Well, how does she take pain?" Because that's part of this occupation. So the one thing I knew was that I was going to be injured if I became a jockey.

I also knew that my mother's fate is her fate. It's not mine or anyone else's. Bill Shoemaker is a classic example of that. I mean he gets paralyzed in an automobile accident after all those years riding. So I just never considered my mom's deal to be my deal.

Patti: I remember the one time Donna was injured and she was tickled to death that she broke her nose. (Patti starts chuckling.)

Donna: Oh yeah! For the fourth time, because the first three times I broke it, all they did was make it go further and further that way (she nods her head to the right). And I had a bigger nose at the time. I had a Meryl Streep type of nose, which is fine. I got no problem with Meryl Streep's kind of nose. But picture it going a quarter of an inch in the wrong direction! (Patti laughs heartily.)

I remember the first time I broke my nose I was galloping a

horse for Van Berg. And that was when it was the worst. I remember thinking: I am not pulling up! Van Berg was in town and he was there. And I was *not* going to pull up the horse. Of course I had to, and right when I did, Van Berg comes over to start screaming about something. And he goes, "And what the hell happened to you?" And I said, "She (the horse) threw her head up." And he says, "Well, goddamn, that wouldn't have happened if you weren't...blah, blah, blah, blah." (Donna and Patti laugh.)

Donna: If you have ever been around Van Berg, then you can picture it. So I got back to the barn and kept galloping, and I never thought, "Oh, I better do something about this." I can't remember the second time I broke it. But the third time, it was a starting-gate accident. And I rode the card (all of the races) that day; it was like the third race on the card. At what point do I run over to first aid and get this looked at?

So I thought, "It'll happen again; hell, it happens all the time, right?" Well, it was about six years later before I broke my nose again. And this time I had a horse go through the inside fence, so people could *all* see it! And so I was able to get my nose straightened out and take a little off the top, and the insurance paid for it. (Donna and Patti laugh together.)

Donna: There were times I would think, "This is *not* that great of a job." I remember one time just making a stupid mistake. It was a bug-girl (apprentice jockey) move, really. I had been riding in

Chicago. And then I came to Kentucky on my way to Florida for winter at Gulfstream. And I was really nervous about riding at Keeneland, because...*It's Keeneland*! And it's the first time I'd ridden in Kentucky.

So opening day I'm on four horses; they all have a little bit of a chance. I win three out of the four races, and I'm second by half a length at 20-1 in the other one. And that horse ended up breaking his foot or he would have won, too. Point being, I get off to this incredible start and I ended up fourth-leading rider at the meet.

I go from there to Churchill Downs for their fall meet, precipitous to the fall meet at Gulfstream. And I went the whole entire fall meet with one win at Churchill. I mean I had had this great high at Keeneland; Lukas rode me on a couple of horses for the first time. And then I have *one* win at Churchill Downs. Now I have to go down to the toughest meet I've ever been to coming off this really bad meet.

But I still had some outfits who really stood behind me: Carl Nafzger, Tom Proctor, David Carroll. And one of the first days I'm there, I'm on this horse of Carl Nafzger's, and I'm on the rail and I'm behind [jockey] Earlie Fires. Earlie Fires has a horse to the outside of him. And we're turning for home. And there's a rule in horse racing — you might as well just write it in stone because it is a *rule* — you always go around two, and you always sit behind three [horses].

It was just stupid for me to go for the sucker move on the rail, but I did because it opened up a little bit, and I wasn't thinking "this guy is Earlie Fires, he's been riding for ninety years, he's *not* going to let me through there." So I fell right into the trap. I would get up in there, a half-length in. And he goes to the left-handed whip, and my horse won't even *think* about running up into that left-handed whip. By now it's too late to take back because the other horse beside him is stopping, and I'd have to lose three lengths to go around him.

So I claimed a foul on Earlie because he'd made it so tight. So when we came back, I said to Earlie, "You're not going to come down (be disqualified). It was a stupid move to begin with." I said, "I fouled just because Carl wanted me to claim foul, but it was just a stupid ride." And Earlie was like, "Don't be so hard on yourself!" And I was just ripping myself, "That was a terrible ride. There's no excuse for a ride like that."

I get back to the girl jocks' room and I was like here I have the chance to make it to the top and what do I do? Worst ride I've made in, like, three years. But everybody does that. It had nothing to do with me being a girl. It had nothing to do with me being a girl trying to prove anything.

Patti: Human error.

Donna: It was just bad timing for it. And, of course, the bad timing always comes when you're putting the worst pressure on yourself because you're really trying to prove something. And, of course, I overcame it.

I remember I would never cry in the jocks' room. I would never cry in front of the guys or the trainers or anybody. But there were times it was all I could do to make it to that shower.

Even when everything *is* going great and Wayne Lukas is riding you and Jerry Romans is riding you and you're getting all these live horses to ride. And Neil Howard just named you on one, and then you go four or five days in a row and twelve favorites run up the track (finish far back).

And I said, "All right, God. Obviously this isn't what you had in mind. I said I'd try it and you said you'd give me some mounts. I get the idea, okay? I quit." And that was it for me. And then I won. I nailed Julio Espinoza, the leading rider, by a nose. And as I was going by he goes, "Good ride!" And I was, "*Yes*! I am meant to do this!" That's how God would always talk to me. I'd go, "Okay, I understand what you're saying." And he'd go, "No, you *don't* understand what I'm saying."

And I think the biggest part about that and the part that I didn't get for so long and then I realized — it's not God giving me ability. It's me understanding, accepting, and using that ability. God gives everybody the ability in their chosen endeavors, or they wouldn't be there.

When I made that terrible ride at Gulfstream, I remember the thought going through my head for the two months preceding it was that Julie Krone wasn't going to Gulfstream because she had hurt herself. And everybody's going, "Well, it's a great year for you to go, Julie's not there and blah, blah, blah." My thoughts preceding all that were, "I hope they don't find out I'm not as good as Julie." Or, "When are they going to find out I'm not as good as they think I am?" And it wasn't until I started saying, "No! I'm every bit as good as that guy or that guy or that girl," that finally all the successes started to come my way. So the point is, God is always there for you. And God always allows you to have it, but you've got to accept it. And you have to feel like you deserve it. And I think that's what happens with me.

Patti: I can say that in most all the races I rode, when I was sitting in the gate, I would always have the thought, "God, let us have a safe trip." I would always have that thought. And with 1,202 winners, you know how many races were run. Many. And I always had that conscious thought. I was at Latonia, which is now Turfway Park. It was 1980, I think, and it was a Sunday card. Going into the first turn, I went down. I got shut off (an opening between horses suddenly closed). I went down and another horse came down over the top of me — it was Melinda Speckart who went down over me.

Jamie Bruin, who was my son-in-law, was absolutely amazed when he heard me say that that was my first spill. And I had been riding bad trash at Waterford and Commodore Downs — bad horses — horses with ankles like this and knees like this. (Patti laughs dryly as she holds her hands in the shape of a balloon.) Jamie was amazed. He had gone down on his seventh mount. I had had horses break down, but I had never gone down. After Donna started riding, there were times that I would get calls, "Mom, you won a race for me last night." I'd say, "What? What did I do?"

Donna: That's true. It would come to me; it would be like an epiphany. One time in particular, I was going into the first turn at

Minnesota (Canterbury Downs) and I had speed, but so did the two horses to the outside of me. And it was like a seven-horse field, and it was, "If I'm not on the lead, I don't win, and if they're not on the lead, they don't win — both of these other two." I'm just thinking, "What is going to happen here? I mean we're going two turns, what are we going?" Twenty (seconds) for the first quarter, you know?

I just think, "Well, I'm going to ride it as it comes up." So I send my horse away from there, and we're all going into the turn and just straight across the track. And suddenly it occurred to me: I do *not* have to turn now (Donna pauses for effect and Patti laughs) just because the turn is there. 'Cause I remember Mom saying, "Just go straight for another jump. And then take a left and you hang them out to dry!" (Patti guffaws.) So I'm going into the turn, and I was like, "One, two — phew!" And they were gone, and I was a length in front of the field, and I won. So I called up Mom that night and said, "By the way, thanks for that little tip."

Patti: This morning I had coffee in the track kitchen with [trainer] Kenny McPeek. You know, Donna rode his first stakes winner.

Donna: He sent her up to Minnesota to run. She has a shot, she's like 6-1, 7-1, and he says, "If you even *think* about making the lead before the head of the lane, I'm going to *kill* you when you come back here. You just get her back and eat her, whatever you have to do to get her back. Do not make the lead before the top of the stretch." And I was like, "Yes, *sir*! Gotcha, Captain." I mean he introduced himself, "Hi, I'm Kenny McPeek. Nice to meet you," and then went off. And he was right. She only had one run, and he had come all that way to Minnesota. He told me he was in the van for sixteen hours.

Patti: This is funny because you would say now that Kenny McPeek is kind of an upper-echelon trainer, right? His first stakes winner he rode Donna. He rode Julie [Krone], and now he has an owner who will not ride girls. At the level of racing I was at, the only thing owners did was pay the bills. I don't know of any owner's interference with anybody.

Donna: The other night at Patti Cooksey's roast (at which Cooksey received an award from a horseracing fan club), Greta Kuntzweiler sent in a comment and what she said was, "And you taught me how to deal with owners: 'Oh, and how *is* your beautiful wife?' " (Both women chuckle.) And it is honestly one of the things that I teach girls to this day — girls that I take an interest in — if you want to ride for an owner, you *better* figure out how to get along with his wife. You better figure out how to get his wife saying, "Why don't we ever ride *her* on any of our horses?" Because they call the shots. Whether the men admit it or not, they call the shots. If you're not on the side of the women, then you're against them. And that's not the side you want to be on.

Donna: The girl jocks' room is a place where you can say anything you want and anybody else can but it doesn't leave that room. And that was kind of the rules. And if there was a girl in there who wasn't going to abide or adhere to those rules, we knew it. And you just didn't talk around her or whatever.

But I mean I can come back in after a race and say "that guy is *such* an asshole" and know that none of those girls is going to walk out and go, "Well, Donna didn't even like riding for you, why do you ride her? Every time you ride her, she says you're an asshole!" (Patti and Donna are laughing.)

So it was that way in there. But at the same time, yes, we did have a camaraderie, and it was somewhat selective. When I came up — not in my mother's day, because she had a lot of jealousy to deal with in the girls' room — the majority of women understood that the better you do, the better I do. If it's good for you, it's good for the rest of us. But at the same time, I never let my agent have another girl rider.

I never wanted it to be, just, "that's the girls." I never would have a girl agent. And I think there've been some really good girl agents who definitely should be considered to be hired, but not by a girl rider. You're just always trying to separate yourself, and at the same time, you have each other. It's such a huge, huge mind game all the time. It's actually like playing chess. It's like if I make this move, what will their move be, and if they make that move, what move would I have to retaliate?

Patti: And looking at agents, I mean this agent could be the leading agent and have the best riders at the best tracks, but has he ever hustled a girl's book? Because it's a different ball game.

Donna: It's all relative to where you are. At Fort Erie the other day, out of a ten-race card, eight of the races were won by women.

Patti: Really?

Donna: It's true, some people are going to ride girls and some people aren't. But others can be persuaded to take a chance. There was a guy named Wilson Brown who I rode for in Minnesota. I had asked my agent, "Let's go by and see Wilson Brown, he's one of the leading trainers." And my agent said, "I saw him the other day and he doesn't ride girl riders." And I said, "Hello? Let's go by and see Wilson Brown, he wins a lot of races."

I went by there the next day, and Wilson said, "Oh, hey, nice to meet you, sweetheart. Your agent was by here yesterday, but I don't ride girls." And I said, "Well, I don't blame you Mr. Brown. I wouldn't ride girls either, but I don't ride like a girl." And he thought that was cute. He ended up riding me on a horse a week later and it won, and I ended up being Wilson's main rider two years later. And you know what he said to me? He said, "You know what I hate about riding you?" And I was like, "Oh no...What, Mr. Brown?" "Every girl rider who passes through stops by my barn thinking I ride girl riders, and *I do not* ride girl riders!"

So there are some men — outfits — who will give it a chance. What people always said about me and Krone is that we had good hands. Nervous filly or a colt who's just a little too smart for his own good, we could figure them out and work with the trainer and get a horse that normally goes to the front end and stops to go along a little bit more.

We worked more with first-time starters. We both worked harder than any of the other guys. Things like that.

That will not change anytime soon; that is always going to be the way it is. In fact there is an apprentice rider coming up now (Kris Prather), and I told her, "You will always have to work hard. Don't think you won't. And it's not going to seem fair, and it isn't. But when all those guys up in New York, or whatever, are staying home 'cause it's too cold out? You better have your ass to work in the morning. Because that's just the way it is."

C H A R L S I E   C A N T E Y

$\mathcal{N}$etwork Natural

When networks began regularly televising American
Thoroughbred races in the 1950s, they relied on a few stationary cameras that showed limited action. Since then, technological advances
have brought us the multi-camera, comprehensive coverage that
allows television viewers to see horses at nearly every angle.

One attempted improvement, though, never got off the ground —
and literally almost put the protagonist on it. The scene was the 1986
Preakness (won by Snow Chief). ABC producers decided to make better use of their versatile and talented color commentator-reporter
Charlsie Cantey, who was one of the first women to play a leading role
in network sports telecasts. Not only would she ride alongside the
jockeys she was interviewing in the post parade and after the race, they
decided, but Cantey would have a small television camera mounted
on her riding helmet so that she could provide on-track views as well.

It was Cantey, an accomplished equestrian and knowledgeable

horsewoman, who had popularized the on-track interview on national television, so she was comfortable with the audio elements of this plan. With her love of racing and desire to promote it, she seemed perfectly suited to this assignment.

"But it turned out to be just too much," Cantey recalled. "I'm going to be the cameraman, and I'm going to be the talent, and I'm going to ride a horse. I'm going to be out there with the Preakness horses, and I am also going to watch where we are going so I don't run into anybody.

"I should have put my foot down and said 'no.' I was riding a pony provided by somebody from Pimlico. Well, whoever tacked up this pony didn't have all the stuff on there right, and all these pounds and pounds of batteries and stuff in the saddlebags start to slip as I'm galloping down the stretch. The stuff was sliding up under this pony's belly and all the wires are pulling my head backwards, and I'm strapped into this helmet. I could have been strangled.

"The race has started and the field is going down the backside. All I could think of was, 'what if I fall off and I'm in a heap on the stretch and the pony is loose when they get over here?' It could have been a freaking disaster. Well, fortunately, I could ride well enough despite the fact that my head was pulled around. I got the pony into the paddock and he is freaking, spinning around in a circle with all this stuff tangled up in his legs. I gathered up all that equipment and took it to the TV truck, and I said, 'I'm never getting on another horse and broadcast again as long as I live.' And I haven't.

Charlsie Cantey's knowledge of horses is reflected in her on-track interviews on national television.

"But you know what?" she said. "Here it is fourteen years later, and people still say, 'And here's Charlsie Cantey — she's the one who rides the horses in the interviews.'"

Laughter punctuates many of the statements made by Cantey, a fifty-five-year-old North Carolina native who now makes her home in Maryland with her husband, Douglas Davidson.

Charlsie is the youngest of Oscar and Mary Dearing's three daughters (her eldest sister is author and television personality Barbara Howar). After graduating from George Washington University in 1968 with a degree in art history, Charlsie headed not to Florence, Paris, or a

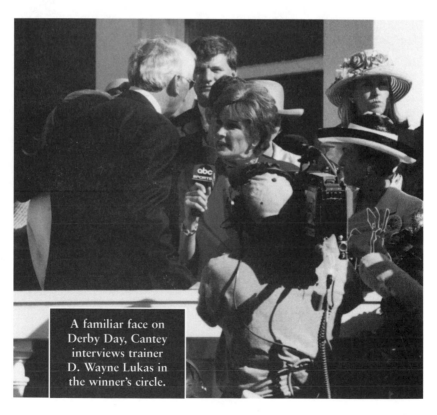

A familiar face on Derby Day, Cantey interviews trainer D. Wayne Lukas in the winner's circle.

New York gallery but immediately for the racetrack, where she got work grooming horses at Delaware Park. In 1969 she married trainer Joe Cantey, from whom she was divorced in 1987; they have a son, Joseph Benjamin Cantey IV (known as J.B.), who is a student at the University of Virginia and a national champion sporting-clay shooter.

Charlsie began her television career in 1975 on WOR in New York City. After a stint as a horse-racing analyst for CBS, she began working for ESPN in 1985 and joined ABC Sports in the same capacity a year later. In 2000 she completed a network trifecta by joining the NBC-TV team for the Breeders' Cup, and in May of 2001 co-hosted the Kentucky Derby coverage for the network. She and her television colleagues have combined to win numerous Eclipse Awards over the years. Cantey also enjoyed a brief but successful training career.

In another life, obviously I must have been deeply involved with horses, because I got right out of the gate in this life just being passionate about them. My family had nothing to do with horses, but I was always interested from the earliest time I can remember. Even if it was a cartoon horse in the Sunday funny papers, I was cutting them out.

I never really saw that many horses early on. I grew up in Raleigh. There really wasn't anywhere you could go to take riding lessons. I remember there was an old mule that used to pull an old four-wheel wagon. The guy would come around to sharpen knives. He would stop right in front of the house, and I would go out there and throw my arms around this mule's legs and just stand there clinging to him until the guy was finished and drove away.

My first memory of a real horse was when I was in first grade. My parents allowed me to go to a small riding academy at Meredith College. They had American Saddle Horses, and they taught saddle seat equitation. It didn't matter to me what it was — it was a horse. I remember the first day they lifted me up and put me on this huge old black horse. His name was Velvet. I can remember to this day sitting in that saddle. They put my feet in the irons, and they said, "Take these reins." And they let me loose. They said, "Okay, now just kind of kick a little bit and he'll walk." Of course, Velvet had broken in a hundred-thousand kids like me. I remember distinctly what it felt like, pulling the rein to the right or the left. I had control over this great big animal. From that day forward, all I wanted to do was be out there all day, every day, riding.

My childhood was not the rosiest. I was sort of a late, unexpected, and not particularly wanted caboose. My two sisters were literally grown and practically gone when I came around. My parents...in those days nobody divorced, but it would have been a whole lot better if they did, but it was too scandalous. Basically, when I look back I wasn't terribly happy. I was terribly insecure — a lot from the unstable home situation. You know, my parents were doing the best they could. They were only trying to survive. I understand how it all happened and why. But that was how it was. It was sort of a lonely childhood. So the horses were the channel out of there and became really the thing that I cared the most about, the thing that validated me.

When I was twelve, I was hoping to have a horse of my own. There was one out there at the riding academy, a kind of reject that nobody really wanted. She was sort of a strange horse and difficult to deal with, but I just loved her and I wanted her. This is when my sister Barbara entered into the picture — Barbara, who was more my mother than my mother.

My father had gone into the hospital for emergency surgery. He was half groggy from the anesthesia, and Barbara said to him, "Now you can see something could happen to you and this child will never have the only thing she ever wants in this world." She just bullied him on his sick bed, and he said, "All right, all right."

So I got this three-hundred-dollar horse, and, believe me, she was my lifeline through my teenage years. This horse became not only my riding horse but my companion — my heart and soul growing up. I knew who I was with the horses, and I am not sure that I knew who I was anywhere else.

Her registered American Saddlebred name was Joy of England's Acres, but we changed it to Dearing's Joy. Dearing is my maiden name. I used to get on her at where we boarded her, and I'd have a little lunch bag. I would ride all over — across Raleigh to the other side of town to my sister's. She was married and had a bunch of kids. I'd go there and jump this horse over the picnic table in the back yard just to entertain the neighborhood kids. I could ride this horse anywhere I wanted to go. She was better than a bicycle, and she was my buddy, my savior.

That was such a feeling of freedom for me. I had that same feeling years later when I was galloping horses at Belmont Park, you know, at 6:30 or 8 in the morning. At Belmont there is a huge hedge all the way down the backside and around the turn, and just outside of that is the Belt Parkway. You could hear the traffic and all these poor slugs driving to work every day, and I'm getting ready to bust one loose at forty miles an hour at the half-mile pole, maybe one that's going to win a grade I this weekend, and I'd think, "I'm so lucky..."

Joy just turned out to be this Cinderella horse. Everything at the riding academy was all hunter-jumper oriented. And here I was with this horse that had a lot of high leg action; she was a Saddlebred. She just didn't fit into the hunter-jumper mold at all. I tried to make a hunter out of her, but it was like trying to make a right-hander out of a left-hander.

One day we were over at a pretty big indoor horse show in Charlotte. During the schooling in the morning, there was a guy who later wound up being an alternate on the Olympic equestrian team. We all had a crush on him. He's schooling a very good mare, and he kept having trouble with one of the jumps.

I'm riding Joy around bareback because I didn't like cleaning tack — I just didn't bother with it. I was kidding this guy, and I said something like, "Having a little problem today?" And he said, "Yeah, and I'd like to see you get that silly-ass looking thing that you're riding to do it."

I was offended — he's talking about my baby! I said to him, "We can do that." And we did. I went over that jump bareback. I can't even believe it now.

A bunch of the kids I knew were watching, and they said, "Oh, my God, you've been doing the wrong thing with her. This is what she needs to be — a jumper." So they literally passed a hunt cap around and collected enough money sitting there on the sidelines to pay my entry fee in the show.

I rode her that night, under the lights with all the painted jumps and all, and it was like a star is born. She was just sailing over those fences. The next night she finished third in the jumper stakes.

For the next four or five years or so, all the way until I went to college, Joy and I went to every show that I could beg, borrow, or steal the entry fee for. We went to the Washington, D.C. International, and she wound up being the Virginia reserve show-jumping champion. I won stuff all over the place with her. She was great. When I went off to college, she was retired.

Going to college, I still spent a lot of time with horses. It's amazing I ever graduated. I used to go down to the big training center at Middleburg (Virginia) to meet my buddies. They were galloping horses. One morning I said, "You're getting paid how much to do this? Where do I sign up?"

After college graduation, I went to Delaware Park where they had a lot of steeplechasing. I was just kind of hanging out with that crew. I was hunting around trying to get a job galloping horses.

Women had no license to ride — there were no women jockeys then. There really weren't that many women around the track; most of them were wives of trainers. I went from barn to barn. It was like, "A woman? No, no thanks. I don't think so."

I knew that I had worked with horses all my life and knew I was a good, hard worker. Some of that comes from the childhood situation where if you work hard enough and if you are really good enough, maybe they will like you this time. So in a sense, I had that kind of built-in psychological twist that made me work harder. It never dawned on me that if I just tried and knocked on enough doors, that I wasn't going to have things work out.

I was sitting in the track kitchen one day, and I was really getting discouraged. Somebody said, "Why don't you go to Frank Whiteley's barn — he is really needing some exercise help." *(Editors' note: Whiteley, the Hall of Fame trainer of such greats as Damascus and Ruffian and Delaware's top trainer, was known for his conservative nature.)*

I said, "Oh, good." I was up and out of my chair and somebody put their hand on my shoulder and said, "Sit down — they're kidding you. Frank Whiteley wouldn't have a girl under his shed row if hell froze over!"

Well, the ironic part of it was that Frank would, and within two or three years I was queen bee exercise rider for Frank and got on all the stars and worked there for ten years.

You know, back then it wasn't a real definite stance — "We've got to hold these women back" — it was more that it didn't cross anyone's mind to have a woman working there.

We sure could have used some sexual harassment rules in those days. There were a lot of remarks and catcalling. It seems like I just ignored it. I just went and did what I did. I wish I could remember how many other girls there were working then. There weren't many; I know that.

The track kitchen at one track I was at back then had virtually a broom closet with a commode in it behind where the kitchen was. That was the only place on that track where a girl could go to the bathroom. Now they have ladies' lounges and ladies' dormitories. Now it's wonderful. But when I started, it was like the Dark Ages. Gosh, I sound like a dinosaur.

Women today probably make up fifty percent of the work force on the backstretch, to say nothing about how so many women are so good at their jobs that they've gone right up the ladder and are valuable assistants and trainers in their own rights. They've shown they can do everything that a man can do.

I don't think we are left with a whole lot of sexual barriers today. I mean, look at somebody like Linda Rice. Now, granted, she's got a strong family connection and she had a leg up, but she is a good horsewoman. She works hard — she knows her stuff — and she never slackens. Nobody cares if you are a male or a female.

It's the same thing in broadcasting. Women are now giving handicapping advice, and men are gathered around the televisions and listening to them. You've got talent like Caton Bredar, people like that, who are just so good. It's become routine.

I galloped Ruffian for Frank Whiteley when she was a two-year-old. Revidere, Honorable Miss, Icecapade, Tiller, Forage, Cutlass — so many good horses.

Ruffian was awesome. We were in Camden (South Carolina) for the winter when she came in. She would have been a yearling when she arrived and turned two that winter. We knew she was well-bred. She was a lovely, strong type, but she was so kind and nice.

They all gallop in groups together down there, and we just all loved her. When somebody would come around looking for a job, Frank would say, "put them on the Reviewer filly" to see how they ride. She was that nice and so intelligent. She was a lovely mover. She worked fast, but she did it so easily it was often very, very hard to tell how fast she was going. That is true of most good horses. They are very good horses, because what they do is so effortless.

But when Ruffian went to the track to work, she just showed herself to be something different, something special. I think everyone expected her to win the first day she ever ran, but I don't think any of us were prepared for the kind of performance she put on. After the second time she ran, there was no denying that she was a great, great filly. *(Editors' note: Ruffian won her debut by fifteen lengths and her next nine starts by an average margin of seven and one-half lengths before her fatal breakdown in the July 6, 1975, match race with Kentucky Derby winner Foolish Pleasure.)*

I started in television in 1975 with WOR in New York. It was a "super station," but it was still basically a local show of New York races. I never looked to do that job. The television people basically came to me. It was never anything I sought, which is the irony of the whole thing. I started with CBS in 1978. It just kind of gathered momentum. The funny part about it is I have a real horror of public speaking. I was asked to emcee the Hall of Fame ceremonies at Saratoga a few years ago and I told them that I simply can't, can't do it. I still get very nervous before a television show.

I had to be one of the first women to be a so-called "expert commentator." What helped me was that the credibility was there for me. I had no problems doing interviews with jockeys. I had probably just worked horses head and head with the same rider that same morning. So they weren't going to roll their eyes and say, "I don't want to do this."

Trainers have changed over the years. In the old days, it used to be, "Don't disturb my horses." I worked for one of the worst along those lines, and his son, too. They would come out of the barn screaming, "Get those goddamn cameras out of here!"

Wayne Lukas was one of the ones that raised the bar for trainers. He's extremely cooperative. I marvel now that some trainers will even pull horses out of their stalls and pose them. I think that's great because racing needs that kind of publicity. We've got to make the owners, the trainers, and the horses believable, recognizable, interesting figures.

A lot of times, and I don't know how to say this modestly, a lot of times we could get an interview because it was somebody who was a friend of mine or somebody who would do it as a favor. I try not to impose on that. And there are times when somebody will just say "no." Not long ago in California, Bobby Frankel had agreed to do an interview; then he just said "no." Bobby and I have been friends since before he was famous. But there are just times when somebody doesn't want to do something. They had me posted with Neil Drysdale (trainer of Kentucky Derby winner Fusaichi Pegasus) through the Derby and Preakness because they knew Neil and I are friends. Sometimes he would turn me down for an interview. That was it. I'd just tell my producer, "Sorry, I did my best." I can't — I simply won't — trade upon friendship.

The hard interview to do — and they have me do this an awful lot — is the losing rider, especially when he's on the beaten favorite. Journalistically, I can see you've got to do it. If the favorite gets beaten in the Derby, you've got to try asking what happened. And I'll tell you what, they amaze me. They are always so forthcoming. Jerry Bailey always kids me when he comes to do a winning interview. He says, "I like these kinds so much better." Basically, ninety-nine percent of the riders are just absolutely wonderful about this.

I don't think the public can ever, ever understand exactly what goes on during a race and how much it takes for jockeys to keep a horse out of trouble and yet still keep him in contention without endangering themselves. I don't think people realize how split-second the danger is out there. We can criticize riders all we want to, but just try it one time. I rode one race in my life. It was at Philadelphia Park; a race for amateur riders. It was a mile and a sixteenth on the turf. The only way I would do it was on the turf. I can't stand getting dirt in my face. It hurts! I don't know how these jocks stand it.

We warm up and get behind the gate. It's a field of twelve; the riders are a whole bunch of other people like me, not jockeys, but amateur-type riders. The head starter comes up and says, "Okay, how many of you have never broken a horse out of the gate?" Three hands went up, one on a rider right next to me, and I said, "Oh, shoot!"

We broke out of the gate, and all I can tell you is the one thing I remember most of all was going, "Wait a minute, the turn is here already!" So now I've lost a bunch of ground around the first turn, and now we're going down the backside and I'm thinking, "That was terrible, I'd better not do that again. Oh, here's another turn!" It was just awful. My horse ran decently, but, believe me, I was just so glad when it was over. I mean, like you're going, "Man, I've got to watch out for this horse in front of me," but then while you are doing that, and watching out for the horses around you, all of a sudden the white rail has turned left and you haven't made the turn. It just went that fast.

I think it was Dave Johnson who interviewed me after the race, and he said, "Well, you've just ridden your first race. What do you think?"

I said, "I think I apologize to every jockey in the United States of America that I have ever criticized."

In 1980 I was pregnant with J.B., so I wasn't riding — for Frank or for television. I wouldn't do anything wrong; I just did everything by the book. Everybody said I was the most boring pregnant person.

My husband then (Joe Cantey) trained this colt, Temperence Hill, who was kind of a late developer. They hadn't even nominated him for the Kentucky Derby. But he'd won the Arkansas Derby, and John Ed Anthony, who owned him, wanted to run him in the Belmont Stakes and he supplemented him. We all thought, "If there was ever a mile and a half horse, it's Temperence Hill."

The night before the Belmont it rained. I remember Joe and I both just lay awake all night listening to the rain and thinking, "Oh, man, Temperence Hill doesn't like the mud." So we were really pretty nervous.

The day of the race I'm doing the CBS show and interviewing Bill Shoemaker in the paddock before the race. He said, "Well, I really like my horse's chances because he's got good tactical speed and he'll be close up. You just can't come from very far back on a track like this, going this far."

Of course, Temperence Hill always came from way back in his races. You could see my face just falling as Shoe says this. Talk about having to be professional!

As the race starts, they've got me positioned up at the head of the stretch, right where they turn for home. So, I'm standing up there and I do my little report on how the horses are warming up and what's going on, and I'm supposed to stay there. That was where I was going to watch the race.

The race starts, and they go down the backside, and I see Temperence Hill is a whole lot closer to the front than normal. I'm thinking, "Oh, man, he's looking good here!"

They come around the turn, Temperence Hill's advancing on the outside, and by the time they go by me he is almost head and head with Genuine Risk. I said, "He's going to win this freaking thing." He's like 52-1.

I just looked at my (CBS) audio guy and I said, "I'm out of here." I'm ripping off headsets and whatever equipment I had on, and I just left and started running. There is a concrete culvert down the outside rail of the track, and all the fans are above me on my right and the racetrack is on my left, and there are horses going by. People are leaning over the rail and they all know me from the show and they are going, "All right, Charlsie, way to go, way to go."

I stopped once because I was so out of breath. I just didn't think I could make it. Then I thought, "I've got to be in this winner's circle...I've GOT to be in this winner's circle." So I go tearing down the rest of the way, and I get there just as they are about to lead the horse in. The joke was that J.B. and I finished third in that Belmont.

All of a sudden somebody grabs me by the arms and hoists me over the outside fence and onto the platform where Jack Whitaker and Frank Wright are doing the CBS broadcast. And I'm still breathing hard, and they're saying, "Congratulations, congratulations, this is great! Did you know he was going to win?"

I never bet. And Joe doesn't bet. But John Ed Anthony bet all the cash he could find. He was so insulted at the long odds on his horse that he kept going back and betting more money. After about the third time he did that, Joe said to him, "John Ed, this isn't Oaklawn Park. Your four- or five-thousand-dollar bet is not going to change the odds on this horse."

John Ed made a lot of money that day. I don't know how much money they left there with. I know they'd bet for a lot of people in Arkansas. They gave Joe Cantey a big clump of cash. It was a day.

I broke all the abstinence rules for pregnant women. J.B. had his first taste of champagne that night. We must have stayed out 'til three in the morning. Our barn was like family; I mean the whole gang of us was out. And when we got home, it was so great. We had a little tiny house in Garden City. There were balloons, signs, flowers, all from the neighbors. It was a day.

I'm away from the racetrack now for the first time in many years — December 31 of 1999 was the last day I had a horse in the barn. I broke my last two-year-old out of the gate the week before that Christmas and was galloping, breezing them myself right up until Christmas.

I trained a public stable for a pretty good short run (beginning in May of 1996). I had some decent horses. I had three stakes winners, two graded stakes-placed fillies. Meaning even more to me was a couple of old cripples I got that some people said, "Look, they tell me this horse is untrainable, but before we give him away see what you can do." And you know, I got them back to the races and won a race or two. I loved training. It was the single most validating thing that I ever did in my life. But it was so hard. It takes every single minute of your time. There is no other life. You simply cannot have another normal life.

My son was thrilled to death when I gave up training. We were talking about it, and I said, "You know, never mind how much I miss the horses, I miss not having butterflies in your stomach because you are doing something competitive, you know? You have to have something like that to kind of work towards." Now J.B. is trying to get me down to the Potomac Boat Club to take up some kind of sculling or rowing or something. He said, "Mom, you could row in the senior women races. You could do it. You could do it!" Know something? He might be right.

But I never set out to do anything other than something in which there was a horse involved. There was never any question in my mind as to whether I could or couldn't do something. If there was a horse involved, I just knew I could.

No matter what it was, whether it was showing, show jumping, galloping horses, training horses, covering races on television, the horse has always been what I'm about. I just did those things because I loved every minute of it. I think that is why everybody on the racetrack is there — they just purely love horses.

CHAPTER 4

JENINE SAHADI

*A*gainst the Odds

F*ew trainers of either sex have accomplished as much in the first eight years of their careers as Jenine Sahadi. She has trained an Eclipse Award winner and won two Breeders' Cup races and a Santa Anita Derby. In 1996 she set a single-season earnings record of $3,458,176 for a female trainer, breaking her own mark set the year before. Yet, this glittering resume has by no means served to guarantee the California horsewoman a barn full of promising prospects.*

"I thought that I would get better horses," she said in her familiar pull-no-punches style, "but in fact I went from winning two Breeders' Cups to a complete professional lull. People just don't want to give horses to women to train."

Sahadi is a member of a prominent racing family. Her father, Fred Sahadi, founded Cardiff Stud Farm, as well as the Barretts Sales Company. Following graduation from the University of Southern California with a degree in journalism/communications, Sahadi worked for seven years in the Hollywood Park publicity and marketing departments. After apprenticing with veteran trainer Julio Canani for two years, Sahadi took out her first license in 1993 and debuted with a bang. She notched her first career win on May 2, won her first stakes race on May 23, and later that season saddled Creston to take the grade III Flying Paster Stakes at Del Mar.

In 1996 Sahadi made racing history when she became the first woman to send out a Breeders' Cup winner: 4-1 favorite Lit de Justice, who captured the million-dollar Sprint at Woodbine and was subsequently voted champion of that division in the Eclipse Award balloting.

The following year, at Hollywood Park, Sahadi again won the Breeders' Cup Sprint, this time with long shot (17-1) Elmhurst, a seven-year-old gelding who had been a maiden two years earlier. Through 2000 Sahadi remained the only woman trainer of a winner on Thoroughbred racing's richest program. (Janet Eliott has trained a winner of the Breeders' Cup Steeplechase, though the jump race has always been held at a different venue and usually on a different day.)

Another singular achievement for Sahadi occurred in March of 2000 with The Deputy's triumph in the Santa Anita Derby. The Deputy, now retired to stud, is partly owned by Team Valor, a partnership also involved in the ownership of the multiple stakes-winning filly Golden Ballet, star of the Sahadi stable early in 2001.

In 1998, Sahadi married fellow trainer Ben Cecil. They make their home in Sierra Madre, California.

Jenine Sahadi has had a career of "firsts" among women trainers.

I don't thrive on adversity, but someone like me who is very out-spoken and only knows how to tell the truth sometimes finds themselves in adverse situations. I put myself in those situations. Because I'm not afraid to put my tush on the line. I'm not afraid to say what I feel is the right thing to say. I'm not really afraid of anything, so I'm considered to be controversial.

Marje Everett (former owner and operator of first Arlington Park, then Hollywood Park) said something to me once that I have remembered ever since I started working for her after I graduated college. She compared men and women in positions of power. She

Sahadi accompanying The Deputy to the paddock at the 2000 Kentucky Derby.

said, "If a man is in the position, he's considered a tough administrator. Women in the same position are considered bitches." And that is so, so true.

I mean, you look at a woman like Marje Everett or a woman like Marge Schott (former owner of the Cincinnati Reds) or Georgia Frontieri (owner of the St. Louis Rams). All of these women are strong personalities. They needed to be strong to get where they did. They made their own decisions. They don't usually rely on other people's opinions.

And a lot of times that's very threatening — not only to men — to a lot of women. Because there are a lot of women out there who have either been raised to be passive or to always agree and go with the flow. I know women who are floored a lot of times by what I say.

I was born January 16, 1963, in Good Samaritan Hospital in Los Angeles. I grew up in northern California. Most of my young life was spent in Los Gatos. My dad started claiming horses in the early 1960s, basically right when I was born. So, I grew up around horses.

My dad is Lebanese. He was born in L.A., grew up in New York. My father is a workaholic, very driven, very tough. He really instilled the work ethic in all of us. We have a really close family. I have two brothers and a sister. I'm the oldest. All four are very successful, independent, doing their own thing.

My mother is from Minnesota; she's Norwegian. She is the sweetest thing that's ever walked the face of the earth. She's beautiful. She is more into doing things in moderation and being sensible, so, you know, it was really a nice (parental) mix. Unfortunately, I don't have a lot of my mother's characteristics. I wish I did. But it's funny because now that she's gotten older and raised four kids, when she's hot about something, she'll call me and ask, "What would you say? What should I do with this?" And that's how I think women have changed over the years. They are trying to be a lot more assertive.

I was a kid who liked to hang out with adults. I was very independent. I always have kind of defied authority. I always thought I was smarter than my teachers. In girls' boarding school, I went through a phase when I didn't want to kneel in church. The Jewish girls didn't have to do it, so why did I have to do it? I was in trouble a lot, prankster-type trouble, funny-type trouble.

That's one thing about me: I love to laugh. I love to crack jokes at some other people's expense. But I only do it to those people that I don't care about. I have to respect somebody in order to like them, and there's a lot of people out there that I don't respect. Consequently, there's a very short list of people that I will even say good morning to. I don't believe in wasting my breath.

After I won back-to-back Breeders' Cup Sprints, virtually nothing happened with my career. In fact, it went so quiet that it was a complete lull. I mean, I didn't have any horses of real consequence.

There's no way that we can rationalize why it happens, because we (women) think we do a good job. We try to do right by the horses. Women do have to work harder. We are always going to be a little bit more controversial. In my case, for the most part, it's always been a first: first Breeders' Cup, first Santa Anita Derby. If you're a woman and competing with men at any sort of level, it's always going to be a first. It's always going to be semi-historical because there isn't any history with women.

There's probably four female trainers here in Southern California compared to about five-hundred men. The numbers would be the same nationwide. It is so much b.s. We talked about this at that University of Arizona symposium (in December 2000). The numbers are completely uneven. And for the most part, women are not given the same quality of stock that men are. If you are given good stock, it's probably because of one main client that you have spent five or six years nurturing and trying to maintain a relationship with. Or it's family money, or your own money, that kind of thing. The thing is, it's just too unfair. No matter what I do, I'm not going to be able to change the perception of those people who feel that women are not capable of training horses.

And if women are going to try to do this, they better be very careful about how they start. You better not start off with two ten-thousand-dollar claiming horses because no one's going to pay you any attention. If you're going to try to take this on — and this is what I tell young girls — start doing it with some ammo. You need to have a plan of attack. You need to have owners who are committed to you, people to fall back on. There are too many women who have said, "I'm going to claim two horses and make a splash." But no one gives a shit. The only thing that people care about are horses that are winning big races and competing at very high levels.

I tell them, "Don't do this by the seat of your pants." I mean, I made sure that the first horse I ran was as close to a cinch as I could find. Because it's a lot better for me to win my first race than it is for me to run a bad fourth, then say, "Well, the horse is going to improve." You need to be very careful about how you start.

Even some of the most prominent women who own racehorses don't give horses to women. There are a lot of women who are in control of racing dynasties, and they don't have any female trainers. I mean, Madeleine Paulson left that horse (K One King) with Akiko Gothard, but I don't think she's ever given her another horse. And she certainly only left the horse there because Akiko had the horse to begin with.

Helen Alexander (of the King Ranch family and owner of Middlebrook Farm)...Virginia Kraft Payson (owner of Payson Stud)...there's a lot of women who control quite a bit of bloodstock, but you don't see them with female trainers. So if they're not doing it, it's kind of hard to believe that a lot of men will. There is definitely an old boys' network that exists. I don't think that it's gotten much better.

Some wives feel threatened by female trainers, okay? Probably more often than not, husbands are running the show. Women don't want to be threatened by a horse trainer. Luckily for me, the people I train for, I am really friendly with their wives, and the wives come to the barn. But that's not my main job. I am not a baby sitter. But, like I said, luckily I don't have that kind of situation now, and I haven't had it in the past.

There's another side of the coin, too, where there are women who are really pushing to give horses to women trainers because they feel women are more nurturing. I got a call the other day from this woman who said, you know, "This horse really seems to respond well to women for whatever reason." She goes, "We might just be totally out there, but my husband and I have talked about it." She was the one who called. It wasn't the husband. We talked for about twenty minutes on the phone. I thought we had a great conversation. Hopefully, she'll send the horse in.

The problem that I have in this industry is I really get along with the animals better than I do the people, because the horses don't talk back to me. I go to bed at night knowing that I've always tried to do right by them. I let the horse tell me when he is ready to run. You have to kind of try to speak another language with them. You can't train horses and not adore them. You have to love animals, and you have to love what you do. There's so many disappointments in this game.

I am very honest when it comes to communicating with my owners. They know what's going on. And I believe in cutting your losses. I always say to people, "I'd rather take my arm off at the elbow than wait and take it off at the shoulder." That sounds like kind of a gross statement, but it rings very true in horse racing because you have to be that way. It's a business.

Owners do this because they enjoy it. Most people don't expect to make any money. But if you're going to assume that maybe eighty percent of the people in the business lose money, you'd like to try to make sure that they at least have some fun in the process.

That brings up the issue about who I train for. I don't want to be in a situation where I can't be myself, or I can't tell the truth; where I can't laugh, or where I can't cut to the chase. So if I get in a bad situation with a client, fortunately for me, this is not the end all. If it ended tomorrow, I have two degrees that I could fall back on. So I want to be in a situation with clients where I can just be myself. If somebody can't handle the truth, then there's other places they can go where they can get the lines of bullshit. It won't come from me.

Owners have to take responsibility for themselves as well. If owners aren't getting the communication (from trainers) they want, it's nobody's fault but their own. Owners have to pay attention. They're responsible for their own destiny, too. I read something in *The Blood-Horse* about people not researching trainers. They'll just throw horses at people...They spend more time researching a car than they do a trainer.

If a horse can't run or can't make it here (in Southern California), I have to call and tell the owners that. If I don't, it's not good for the horse. It's not good for my help. It's not good for the owner.

Would I get more good horses if my personality were different?

Well, no, I don't think so. Because (trainer) Summer Mayberry is like the sweetest girl that's ever walked the face of the earth. If you're going to find an individual — male or female — who has been more involved in horse racing than Summer Mayberry, be my guest. Go ahead and try to find one. I mean, her (late) father Brian, mother Jeanie, her sister April, they've all been around racing all their lives. And Summer is the sweetest individual.

She does a terrific job. Her horses look great. But she struggles to get horses. If anybody had a license to make it, it should be her. I mean, she gets by, but nobody's walking up and handing her good horses.

When I had that lull after the Breeders' Cup wins, it was so quiet I was ready to quit. Then all of a sudden, Team Valor and Gary Barber popped up and they said, basically, "Okay, here's some horses. Deal with them." It was like I'd hoped and prayed somebody like them would show up to pick my barn up, and they did. And one of the horses was The Deputy.

That changed everything. Before that, I had little faith in the stock I had. And when you go from winning big races — well, the media is brutal. They just annihilate you. I went through a slump when I was like zero for ninety or something like that. I've seen other people go through slumps, and they (the media) aren't nearly as harsh as on somebody who's won a Breeders' Cup. The thing to remember is that I'm only as good as the horses I have. If I've got a bunch of shit in my barn, there's nothing that I can do to make those horses better than they are. I can do what I can to bring out the best in them. But if it's not there, there's nothing I can do.

(Editors' note: Two days prior to the running of the Santa Anita Derby in 2000, Sahadi made headlines in the racing press after an incident with fellow trainer Bob Baffert.

Sahadi and Baffert were seated at opposite ends of a long table at a breakfast press gathering for Santa Anita Derby participants. Among the entrants were Sahadi's trainee The Deputy, who would win the race, and Captain Steve, conditioned by Baffert, who would finish third. The two trainers were being interviewed at the same time. In the midst of the questions, Baffert said to jockey Chris McCarron, regular rider of The Deputy, "By the way, who's training The Deputy, you or Jenine?"

Sahadi responded, "Thank God my horse has a lot of class, because there are a lot of people here who don't have any." She then abruptly left the podium.)

I really haven't talked about it (the incident with Baffert) since the day it happened. I wouldn't address it in Kentucky (in the days prior to the 2000 Derby). I guess there was one day that he called me a chick, and the media came running to tell me "he just called you a chick." They were trying to get a rise out of me, and I didn't bite.

Yes, I was angry the day it happened at Santa Anita. And, no, I did not think for a second that I should just maintain my composure and let it go, that I should be really cool about it. It's not in me to do that. I was shocked. I was pissed, and I had to let everybody know I was pissed. And it's funny because that little incident was newsworthy for about three months. And the only reason it was newsworthy is because I stuck it back to him. If I had just sat there very passively and said nothing, it would have been, "Oh, isn't Baffert being funny?"

I clearly had been pushed to the brink. I was sick of reading all the same b.s. year after year about how someone else is responsible for my career. I did let it get to me for a long time. I went through a phase where I tried to ignore it. Then I learned that that is counterproductive, and now I really do try to defend myself and women in situations where I think that there's a forum for it.

What he (Baffert) said was in a public forum in front of a lot of members of the media. Consequently, I reacted in the only way that I know how. I don't think that I was out of line. I didn't utter profanities. I didn't, you know, start throwing a tizzy fit. I just handled it the way that I thought was most appropriate. I have to defend myself. I can't change the fact that he's a very insecure man.

You know, that whole thing wound up being very positive for me. It didn't get me any new horses to train, but it was a positive. The day of the Santa Anita Derby, even before the race was run, the reception that I got from the people in the paddock, I was almost crying. I mean, these people were so supportive of me. The cheers after the race…it was great. I had never felt anything like that — they were cheering the horse and they were cheering for me. And they were throwing some funny lines at Baffert, too, like "who's training your horse, Bob?"

The Deputy's win in that race was probably the most rewarding win of my career. The Santa Anita Derby means a lot — not just as a major prep for the Kentucky Derby, but for a Californian. And some people had underestimated the horse. They didn't understand the class he had. That horse was truly amazing. I had never been around a young horse like that. He walked off the van at Churchill Downs like a ten-year-old. Every day was just such a pleasure with him.

The Deputy was a big contrast in temperament to Lit de Justice. That horse made me pull my hair out. I do enjoy a challenge like that, too. But you were scared every day you put a saddle on that horse. You were worried he was going to run himself into a fence, or cause an injury to a jockey or to the exercise rider, or pin the groom in the corner of the stall. Lit de Justice wasn't a mean or vicious horse, but he was a very good-feeling horse who had a mind of his own, and he wasn't going to be told anything.

One thing I learned early with Lit de Justice was that you never fight with a horse like that. You will always end up on the ground if you do. You have to go with the flow. If he wants to go left instead of right, you let him go left. If you're trying to fight with a horse, you're always going to be hurt before the horse is. They're a lot bigger and stronger, and nine times out of ten they're smarter than we are.

I've got some two-year-olds now. I don't typically get two-year-olds. I've had a lot of older horses. I love running old horses like (multiple stakes winner) Megan's Interco. A horse's longevity is a statement and a testament to the home that horse has lived in. If I can have a horse like Megan's Interco race until he's ten and make a million dollars, those kinds of things make me proud. My whole thing is trying to do right by the horse. I'm not saying that I'm a saint and that I don't ever make mistakes and that I don't do anything wrong, but I am very conscious of the fact that you need to always do right by the horse.

The toughest part of the game is definitely injuries to horses. I become attached to a lot of these horses. When it became apparent that Elmhurst had to be retired because he was not as good as he was, and Megan's Interco, who was my favorite horse of all time, it's hard. When you go to bed at night and your best horse, The Deputy, is fine, and the next day the horse is basically bowed and retired and finished, that is the hardest part of this game.

When something you feel passionate about ends, you feel bad for yourself, but you also feel horrible for the guy that's been working with the horse for years, and the exercise rider and the hotwalker that, you know, adore the horse. You feel bad for the owners certainly, but you feel bad for the people that are involved with these horses day to day, because for them it's devastating. Most of these people have been with me from the day I started training. Other than the horses, my employees are number one. I'm so grateful to them for the job they do. They are really the unsung heroes.

I think racing is at a crossroads because I don't think we're paying attention to the things that are truly important. We concentrate so much on things that don't really mean anything. The real stories are back here in the barn area — the guys who have worked here for the last thirty years of their lives.

My pet peeve in racing is that if you're going to be involved, be genuine and really follow through with your horses. You have a responsibility the minute you sign a (sales) ticket on a baby. They're not here to solely provide you with entertainment. And the way they're treated shouldn't be governed by the mighty dollar. Follow through with them and be conscious of trying to find them good homes.

The answer isn't always run for a tag and lose them and let someone else worry about it. I see horses that have made $500,000 or $600,000, and people are running these horses for $12,500 up north and they're crippled. You know what? You've made your money. Do right by the horse and find him a home. Don't run him into the ground until he snaps his leg off.

CHAPTER 5

ALICE CHANDLER

*I*n Her Father's Image

*S*he might scoff at being called the doyenne of the Kentucky Thoroughbred breeding establishment, but in the opinion of many, Alice Chandler — daughter of the legendary horseman and entrepreneur Hal Price Headley, and herself for decades a powerful figure in the industry — qualifies emphatically for that unofficial title.

Chandler was born Alice Headley in 1928. Reared on her father's four-thousand-acre Beaumont Farm, she grew up alongside horses. Her ties continue today through her Mill Ridge Farm, a 1,050-acre spread just outside of Lexington.

Hal Price Headley, who bred eighty-eight stakes winners, was a co-founder of Keeneland Race Course and served as its first president. Since 1981 Chandler has been a director of this not-for-profit operation that annually offers two short but high-quality race meets, one in the spring and one in the fall, and hosts the world's most famous horse auctions.

Other influential posts she has held include membership in The Jockey Club and presidency of the Kentucky Owners and Breeders Association. In 2000 she was appointed to the Kentucky Racing Commission and also was honored by the Lexington chapter of the National Association of Women Business Owners with its Winner's Circle Award.

After her father died in 1962, Chandler inherited Mill Ridge and took over its operation. She made her own mark by breeding and then selling a $42,000 yearling who went on, as Sir Ivor, to become the 1968 English Derby winner and Horse of the Year, and a champion in Ireland and France as well. Most recently she sold a $1.5-million colt by Gone West at the Keeneland September yearling sale of 2000.

The second weekend of June 2000 proved a memorable one for Mill Ridge when stallions standing there were represented by an international classic double. Commendable, a son of Gone West, won the Belmont Stakes, and Love Divine, a daughter of Diesis, captured the English Oaks. (In December, Commendable joined his sire in the Mill Ridge stud barn.)

Chandler has four children: two from an early marriage and two from her marriage to Reynolds Bell, who adopted his wife's elder children. Three of the four children are in the family profession: Mike as a trainer, Reynolds Jr. and Headley as bloodstock agents. Since 1972, Chandler has been married to John Chandler, a veterinarian and native of South Africa. The Chandlers make their home at Mill Ridge.

Alice Chandler's racing roots are deeply embedded in the Blue Grass.

Growing up, I didn't have any girlfriends. I was the fourth daughter. Daddy had three daughters from a previous marriage; his first wife died of pneumonia. My mother was his second wife. The three older girls are my half sisters. I was the first child of the second litter (her brother, Hal Price Headley Jr., is also a Keeneland director). Early on I showed him I loved horses. It was easy — I did love horses. Later on, I grew to love and appreciate the land like he did.

When Daddy was building Keeneland, if my toe wasn't underneath his heel I was running way behind. I was eight years old. He never made a fuss of me being a girl. My sisters weren't interested, but I was fascinated with horses early on. I adored Daddy; I idolized him. Wherever he went that I could go, I went.

In the summer when school was out, we used to have breakfast in the Keeneland kitchen every morning. At that point Keeneland couldn't afford to have any suitable dishes. We had soft-boiled eggs served in water glasses, things like that. It's hard to believe it now.

That was during the Depression. Daddy and Louie Beard faced a deadline to get racing started at Keeneland by the fall of 1936. Daddy loaned Keeneland all the equipment he could let them have — all the tractors, all the mules. I rode my pony, Pal, from Beaumont down Versailles Road to Keeneland to watch the work as it went on. It was imperative that they get this going before October.

At four o'clock every morning I was at Keeneland. We had a great time. If there was angst on Daddy's part, I didn't see it. He just worked harder, and he worked everybody else harder. And we got it open on time.

Through that whole first race meet Daddy would add up the betting after every race to see if they could keep the track open the next day. That's how close it was. The Depression was huge.

We sold a lot of life memberships for five-hundred dollars in the Keeneland Club. A lot of the memberships came from Cincinnati. Any way we could raise money we did. Louie Beard was big on that. He was the farm manager for (John Hay) Jock Whitney (Greentree Stud). Louie raised a lot of money out of the East and got a lot of people interested.

Chandler with her beloved father Hal Price Headley, a founder of Keeneland Race Course.

Daddy and Louie were a very good pair. Daddy was the roll up your sleeves and get dirty type. Louie was more go out in his suit and have lunch. Anyway, they made Keeneland work.

My father turned me loose on the farm. In the summertime, I never came home until dinner time. On the farm there were a lot of men, workers. I guess I had people watching over me that I didn't even know about. It's a wonder I didn't grow up to be more spoiled rotten than I am.

I had a super pony named Pal that I spent all day with. Sometimes more time than that. One time, when I was four years old, my parents had gone out to some party. There was a nanny who was supposed to be watching me. I snuck out on her, and they finally found me in the barn, asleep with Pal, curled up between all four of his legs. I remember that happening very well.

I broke my wrist jumping with Pal because my sister had parked her bicycle on the other side of the jump where I couldn't see it. I was eight. The fall knocked me out. When I came to, I was sitting on Daddy's lap in Beaumont House. He was always there for me if I got in trouble.

One of the things I learned from the men who worked on the farm was how to shoot craps. They were good at it because that's what they did during their lunchtime — shoot craps.

There was a race rider named (William) Smokey Saunders who had won the Triple Crown on Omaha in 1935. He came to ride for my father. The first time I ever saw Smokey I was nine years old and he turned the corner in front of the barn that the craps game was in.

I was running around the paddock on my pony. He stopped and he said, "Are you trying to jump the fence?" I was highly unamused. And I said, "Absolutely not. And who are you?" He introduced himself. We got to be good friends. He was twenty-one years old.

Smokey was the one I cleaned out in the craps game. It was just one of those things. I mean, you get red hot, and you make all these passes. We kept raising the stakes. I couldn't lose. I won six-hundred dollars and Smokey Saunders' car. All the guys in the barn, the grooms, were watching. After it was over, the only thing I did was when I went home to lunch I bragged to Daddy that I had won Smokey Saunders' car. And Daddy said, "Give it back." He was trying not to laugh. So I gave the car back.

When I was young, I never felt I had to go anywhere because everything I wanted or needed was right here. Now my mother, bless her heart, decided when I was twelve that I really needed to go away. She had culture; she was very well-educated; she was a pretty neat lady. She has gotten left behind in some of my discussions, but she was a big part of me.

So she sent me to the Convent of the Sacred Heart School in Cincinnati. They'd never seen a pony or a horse there. That was a long winter for me. The nuns taught me not to butcher the King's English and a few other things. When I got out of there, my mother sent me to Warrenton Country Day [School] in Virginia. That was when I was fifteen, and I stayed there a year and a half. I never went to college. My father just didn't think college was necessary.

He went to Princeton for two years, but then his father had a stroke, and he had to come home. But for women, he thought college was totally unnecessary.

When my son Mike went to the University of Kentucky, after about three weeks he came to me and he said, "Mom, I know an education is important. But I can't handle this. I really want to train horses." I told him, "All I can say to you is, that's fine, but do me a favor: pick the best people to go to and learn from." So he ended up with (Hall of Fame trainer) Frank Whiteley Jr. And Frank Whiteley ended up being to him the father he never really had. Mike made a great choice.

My son Reynolds graduated from UK and married and went to Florida and worked on a farm. He called me up one day, this was in 1975, and said to me, "I know I need you, and I think you need me." So I said, "Come back." So he got to be the general manager here at Mill Ridge. He was the general manager for fifteen years. Then he started his own bloodstock agency. He's done very well.

My other son, Headley, went to Vanderbilt. When my friend Bill O'Neill and I decided we should start up a bloodstock agency — we named it Nicoma, after a favorite mare of mine — Bill said, "Who are we going to get to run this thing? It won't be either you or me." So I got Headley to run it, and it's doing very well, too.

In contrast, my daughter Tish (Patricia Houston) has no involvement in the horse business at all. She works for an interior decorator in Lexington.

The memories I have of Daddy, he would have been good at anything he tried. He was highly motivated; he had a ton of common sense, which is really important. He lived three lifetimes in seventy-three years. Everywhere he went he kicked up the rugs. I mean, he did not dawdle.

When I was growing up, there were a lot of independent, large absentee landlords with farms here. The Whitneys, the Wideners, the Vanderbilts. We didn't race in the wintertime. Daddy bought ten-thousand acres near Albany, Georgia, named Pine Bloom, and he built a twenty-six-stall barn and a three-quarter-mile training track. He loved to hunt. There were quail down there and turkeys and all that good stuff, so he used to go down there right after the Keeneland meeting ended in October, and he would come back in the middle of March ready for the Keeneland spring meeting opening. And all of his two-year-olds would be ready to run.

He'd train the two-year-olds down there in the good old Georgia sunshine, and they'd come home with no names on their halters. They'd just have numbers on them. Daddy didn't want people to know their names before they raced. Daddy loved to bet. The idea was you'd sit on something you thought was going to be a barn burner, then you turned him loose. Keeneland was the first place they'd start their two-year-olds each spring.

One day at Saratoga he won eight-thousand dollars. He gave it to Duval Headley (Hal Price's nephew and Alice's cousin) to keep [overnight]. Duval was training for him. Duval was rooming with Bull Hancock (Claiborne Farm owner Arthur B. Hancock Jr.) up there. They were supposed to sit on that money all night long. And they put it under a pillow where they were staying in one of those little cottages, and they stayed there all night without going out. They were to keep it until Daddy could take it to the bank the next morning. So they did. Daddy didn't like to have money lying around. As I said, he loved to bet, and he was good at it. But when they got the pari-mutuel takeout up to ten percent, he quit betting.

For years when Keeneland opened in the spring, there was just sort of an unannounced agreement between trainers and owners that when you first came back after no winter racing, and after all your winter training and boarding bills had piled up, you were allowed to take a shot in a claiming race with a drop-down horse (one descending in class) in order to try to win a purse, and nobody would claim that horse from you. It was a nice thing. That was back when racing was smaller. It's gotten too big now to have that go on.

I think there are still some of the traces of guys taking care of each other like they did years ago. Mike (her son) is stabled in a barn down there at Churchill that Indian Charlie (racing newsletter writer-publisher Ed Musselman) calls "The Ghetto." Mitch Shirota (a former jockey) has been stabled there, too. He won a stakes at Keeneland last fall. Everybody just went berserk. Indian Charlie had printed up a sign saying that Mitch's horse, Jadada, was going to win the race. After he did win it, crowds of people were there holding the cardboard sign up for the winner's circle photograph. That kind of thing was very, very common in the old days. But the game has gotten so big and impersonal that we don't see much of that anymore. It's too bad.

I was born with a passion for horses. I had certain favorites, certainly. My pony, Pal, was one. So was a filly named Hipparete. She was a full sister to Menow, a champion that Daddy bred. Hipparete was crooked (ill-formed legs). Daddy didn't think she would ever stand training, so he gave her to me as a two-year-old. Was I happy to get her? Oh, I fell in love with her. I liked her because she was bred so well and because she was so kind. Louie Beard bet me ten dollars that she would never win a race. I enjoyed being paid off by Louie. She wound up winning four races and producing three stakes winners.

Hipparete used to get out of her stall at night. She'd reach out and somehow unlatch her stall door. I would find her in the morning in the barn, visiting with the other horses. She had a lot of personality. She also wound up as a foundation mare. She was the dam or ancestress of all kinds of good stakes winners.

Daddy's foundation mare was Alcibiades. She was the dam of Menow. Alcibiades is the fourth dam of Sir Ivor. He was the first stakes winner that I bred and sold. I'd bred them before, but I'd never had to sell them. I had to sell Sir Ivor, because when Daddy died, there wasn't any money. Daddy was in the process of building the place up again when he died. He left me four mares. I had to go into the boarding business. Bull Hancock was a friend, and he helped me get clients. I borrowed the money from my mother to finish the barn that was under construction.

Sir Ivor was by Sir Gaylord out of the mare Attica. I was always crazy about Sir Gaylord. He broke down on the eve of the Kentucky Derby, for which he was favored. He was a beautiful-looking horse, and he had a good temperament. Attica's sire was Mr. Trouble. He was a very aptly named horse. Mr. Trouble was the only horse that, like Daddy said, "tried to commit suicide every day of his life." But Sir Gaylord's temperament won out.

Sir Ivor was a May 5 foal, a big, tall, kind of slab-sided horse. We had trouble foaling him. We had pulled and pulled and pulled and couldn't get this foal out of Attica. So I went screaming out of the foaling barn and up to the house and got Reynolds out of bed. He was fifteen years old. He got out of bed — very reluctantly — and he went down there and gave one pull and that was it. The foal came out.

Sir Ivor turned out to be a very sensible horse. I guess he flew in airplanes about twenty times. He loved attention, and he loved to get his tongue pulled, even for years when he was a stud horse.

Sir Ivor was bought for $42,000 at Keeneland by Raymond Guest. He was the ambassador to Ireland then, and he sent Sir Ivor to Ireland to be trained by Vincent O'Brien (widely known as "The Wizard of Tipperary"). When Sir Ivor ran in the Epsom Derby, we went over — my mother, my son Mike. It was the first trip overseas for Mike and I. We all got fancy clothes for the trip. Mike was twenty-one. My mother wasn't young then, but she was great.

We stayed at Claridges in London. I was shocked when we got to England and found out that Vincent hadn't worked this horse a mile before the race. Because my concern was that Sir Ivor wouldn't go a mile and a half (distance of the Epsom Derby) because of the way he was bred. But I forgot that his dam was by Mr. Trouble, who was by Mahmoud (the 1936 Epsom Derby winner), so we had some distance in there.

At Epsom we sat in Raymond Guest's box. Bull Hancock was there, Jim Brady, Mike, my mother. We're watching the race, and Sir Ivor is down on the rail. Mike is standing up on a chair behind us in his top hat and morning suit, and all of a sudden the chair breaks out from under him. By the end of the race, Mike is off the chair and just hanging from a beam so he could see. He stayed up there until the race was over.

At the eighth-pole, I said to Bull, "We're beat." He didn't disagree. Then I said, "He's going to be fourth." By this time Lester (Piggott) had gotten him out, and Sir Ivor was rolling. And I said, "He's gonna win it!" And there he was. Thanks to Lester Piggott, who is the greatest jockey I've ever seen.

You know, at the time I thought, "This is easy. This bus comes along every fourteen minutes." I learned better later on.

I also didn't realize at the time it was going to help so much in the future.

The biggest difference Sir Ivor made was in the Keeneland sales, because he was the first really good horse that had ever been bought there and gone across the ocean and succeeded. That's what brought the people — the Europeans, later the Arabs, the Japanese, many other people — to the Keeneland sales. That's really what happened.

I don't think that being a woman in a man's world was a disadvantage. I truly don't. But I never really went out to play the feminine card. I don't know, they (men) just sort of accepted me. It's nice to be on the Keeneland executive board as a woman, because I'm one of the guys. Maybe I was so stupid I never knew it was a disadvantage, being a woman in this business. I just thought, "I can do it. I'm as good as they are."

I'm honored to be a part of Keeneland. That's where Daddy died, you know. He had worked all the horses that morning. They had just come up from Georgia; there were twenty-four horses. We had to get them ready to run in two weeks when the meeting opened. He watched them from over at the five-eighths pole. I was in the grandstand. He shouldn't have been doing what he was doing, because he'd had some heart trouble.

We came back to the barn. He and I were sitting in the tack room discussing the works. He'd been having some chest pains — every morning around eleven o'clock. He all of a sudden got up, with no explanation, and walked out of the tack room. The door had one of those drop-down latches on the outside, and I found I was locked in the tack room. I couldn't get out.

Daddy went down the shed row, all the way to the bottom, to look at the horses and talk to the men. He came back, and two stalls from the tack room there was a filly named Trouble Spot. My son Mike was holding her over the webbing because the groom was putting her bandages on. And Daddy said to Mike, "Son, I don't feel very good. Will you hold me?"

Well, it's a terrible decision for a horseman to make — to let go of a shank on a horse for any reason. But Mike dropped the shank and when he reached for Daddy, Daddy slipped right down between his hands and he was dead before he hit the ground.

I was still locked in the tack room. I think Daddy knew what was going to happen. He didn't want me to see it. After Mike let me out, I must have walked five-hundred laps around that barn, waiting for them to come and get Daddy.

After Daddy died, I cried on Hipparete — the crooked-legged filly he gave me when I was eighteen — for about a month. She was eighteen that year; this was in 1962.

Anyway, he was a hell of a fellow. I wish he could come back for just a day to see what Keeneland is like now. But, of course, I'd never be able to let him go back after just one day.

F R A N C E S C A (M A R I A) R A B A D A N

Spit and Polish

T*he U.S. Census Bureau in March of 2001 reported the nation's Hispanic population at 35.3 million, an increase of fifty-eight percent since 1990. This huge jump is powerfully reflected in the ethnic make-up of the work force on backstretches of Thoroughbred racetracks all over the country, particularly in Chicago. According to an official of the Chicago-based Illinois Thoroughbred Horsemen's Association, about ninety percent of backstretch workers are of Mexican descent.*

Many of those workers are women, and among them is Francesca "Maria" Rabadan, a mother of eleven who grooms horses for trainer Gene Cilio.

Born in Guerrero, Mexico, in 1949, she came to this country in 1985. Her first job here was as a migrant worker in Florida. In 1990, she moved to Chicago and began working for trainer Herschel Allen at Arlington Park, where she began grooming horses. Subsequently she was employed as a groom by trainers Noel Hickey and Merrill Scherer

Francesca Rabadan treats her charges as if they were her children.

before signing on with Cilio in 1998. She has been with Cilio since then. Rabadan makes her home in Cicero with her two youngest children, both high school students, and Andres Contreras, a night watchman at Hawthorne and her companion of the past fourteen years.

The groom's role in racing is often not appreciated by outsiders, but insiders know that few horses can overcome a bad groom anymore than they can overcome a bad ride. As the hands-on caretakers of these expensive Thoroughbreds, grooms are required to bathe and brush their horses; "do them up," which involves putting on bandages, applying liniment, and cleaning feet; and feed and water them. Grooms also clean equipment, tidy up the shed row, and alert the trainer to any changes in the mental and physical condition of their charges.

Those are the basic job requirements. As the horses' most constant companions — either while shipping from track to track or walking between the stall and the track — grooms influence their horse's mental well-being. A contented horse is one tended by a caring, conscientious groom, and its level of contentment is almost invariably reflected in racetrack performance.

On a cold, rainy February morning at Hawthorne Race Course — as horses nibbled at their hay racks and sparrows chattered overhead in the steel rafters of Barn F — Rabadan interrupted her raking of the already neat shed row floor to talk of her life in racing. Serving to translate her words from Spanish to English was Joaquin Cambray of the Illinois Thoroughbred Horsemen's Association staff.

I get up at two in the morning. I am the only woman in the house, so I get up early and I sweep, I mop, do the dishes, and then I am ready. I get to the barn at 3 or 3:30. I come shouting to my fillies and my horses when I arrive; "Mama" to the fillies over here, "Papa" to the horses over there.

Horses get attached to people, yes. I have a mare that if I give her a bath, she lets me; she is very good. But if a man gives her a bath, well! She kicks all over the place and complains a lot. I teach my horses to be very gentle. I like them as though they were my children.

My name is Francesca Rabadan. The first boss that I had when I arrived here (in Chicago) couldn't say my name, and he is the one that named me Maria. Now everybody knows me as Maria, even those down in Guerrero where I am from. When they call me on the phone, they ask for Maria.

My life was very sad. My mother died when I was born. My father died later. I only found out when I was eighteen that the person who raised me wasn't my mother. But I think of that person as my real mother. She is an old woman and lives in Cuernavaca, and I haven't stopped supporting her. Sometimes she gets sick, and I have to send her whatever she needs to get better.

I never went to school. I don't know how to read. I struggled a lot in Mexico. That's why I decided to come here. My children [already] were all born then. They were all born alone, with just me there. I would close the door, and I had them all alone.

My husband never helped me at all with the kids. I had to be father and mother to my children. I used to work in the country. I had to deal with my children; I took care of everything because that man was a bum all his life…drinking and gambling and all that. He never helped me with the kids at all. I raised them by myself.

When I left Mexico, it was in 1985. I had to leave my children there with relatives. I brought them five years later. One of the kids, a boy, was a month-old baby when I left. He is seventeen now. One of my daughters, the oldest one in the family, took care of that child. She had an eleven-month-old child but stopped nursing her baby to nurse her little brother. My daughter's name is Guillermina Sanchez.

I came across [the border] with a cousin. First we went to Phoenix, and from Phoenix I went to Florida, and from Florida I came to Arlington. By the grace of God I didn't suffer at all on the way.

In Florida I worked in the fields. All my life before then I worked in the fields. I worked on picking tomatoes, picking cucumbers, picking sweet peppers, picking squash, picking watermelon. Watermelon was hard…forget it! And you have to lift and carry the baskets full of tomatoes to the trucks. The work is very hard, and it's very hot there.

You have to work by contract there. I started at seven in the morning, and I didn't have water until one in the afternoon, just so I didn't waste any time. I was running all the time. Once, when I went for a glass of water, I fell. At 2:30 [in the afternoon] I woke up in the hospital. They took me half dead from work to the hospital. Ever since then I've been bothered by the heat. Whenever it's hot here, I get sick…it's like I get dehydrated…ever since that time in Florida I've been affected.

In 1990 I came to Chicago. There was someone from Florida who was coming, a family also from Guerrero; they came to Arlington. I came with them. That's how I ended up here with the horses.

My first boss was Herschel Allen. I only walked horses for a month; then I started grooming. I learned it by myself. At that time there were almost no Mexicans here, and the ones that were here, how could I expect to ask them for a favor? I suffered a lot at first. It cost me many tears. I couldn't understand what they were telling me. I would start crying. I had no idea where anything was, what I was supposed to do, who I was going to ask. But I had to do it out of necessity.

Later in that year my children came. The oldest of my boys brought them. I sent them the money. They crossed through Nogales, where the coyote (a guide hired to smuggle immigrants across the border into the United States) went to pick them up and took them right to his house. My children didn't suffer. God himself helped me; my children did not have any problems. Some have married and stayed; some are in Florida and California; some have gone back to Mexico.

The year that my children got here, I struggled a lot. I had to work; I had to take my children to school. Then I had to come back to finish working, then go to pick them up. All my life was running because I didn't have any other choice. But that's what I wanted. Since I don't know much, I wanted my children to learn.

God helped me. When I got to Chicago, I found some bosses that looked after me as if they were my parents. After I worked for Herschel Allen, I worked for Merrill Scherer. Among the ones I took care of for Merrill Scherer there was a special horse that I spoiled, (stakes winner) Little Bro Lantis. He was so delicate…tame…but if you talked to him angrily, he went crazy. When I used to give him a bath, I called him "Daddy," and he'd be very quiet, so quiet that even my sons used to get underneath him and stretch their arms out and he did not mind. I got along very well with that horse.

But when Merrill Scherer took his horses away (to other tracks), he took away Little Bro Lantis, which cost me a lot of tears. Merrill Scherer himself told me that I should get a boss that stays here (has horses in Chicago year around), so that I'll be guaranteed my rooms…where I live. If you aren't working, you don't have a room; then my children wouldn't have any place to live. So then I went to work for Gene Cilio.

When I began to work here, there were hardly any Hispanic women. Now there are a lot. We Mexicans, since we came to work here with the horses, we've always worked really hard. We don't care what time we have to get up…we work in all kinds of weather…There are a lot of people that say, "No, it's too cold, no it's late, and I'm leaving…" But we Mexicans can stand all the work the boss gives us.

I don't think life here is more difficult for women than men. It depends on how the woman behaves. In Gene Cilio's barn all the women who work have their husbands working here, too. The only time there are problems is if a woman doesn't behave right.

I am the groom for five horses. They take me all morning. I am finished with my five by 11 or 11:30. Oh, my God (laughs), if I ever only had four horses I would get lazy. I always had five horses wherever I work.

There are eight grooms here with Gene Cilio: Abel, Jaime, Mauricio, Pedro, the other Jaime, Hugo, the guy they call Blondie. I am the only woman, but there are a lot of women hotwalkers. We get along fine together. The others are almost all from the same family from the same town (in Mexico). If there are any problems, we help each other out.

There are all kinds of grooms. Some of them don't love horses, and they just do their work and leave. If the horses don't come back (from the track) by quitting time, they leave. But not me — I am all the time asking, "When is my horse coming? When is my mare coming?" I am always asking after my horses because I like them. The people that work here with us, with Gene Cilio, they are careful. The people that work here don't hit the horses; they get along with them.

All of us grooms have "partners." My partner is Abel. When there is no racing here (when part of trainer Cilio's stable is at the Fair Grounds, the remainder are left at Hawthorne for the winter with assistant trainer Andy Hansen), every other day one of us comes back to work in the afternoon. Abel comes one day; I come the next.

But it is different when there is racing, because if one of my horses is running, both of us are here in the afternoon. My partner has to take care of the stall; he has to put out water for washing the horse. I go out to the track with the horse. If his horse is running, I do that for him. When the horse comes here after the race, we wash him together. If one of my horses is racing, I have to stay late in the afternoon. If they are in the last race, I get home at 6 or 6:30.

When I get to work early in the morning, first I take the bandages off my horses; then I clean their stalls. When I finish the stalls, then I clean my washtubs. I brush (the horses) so that all five of them are ready when they need to start to go out (to the racetrack for morning exercise). I don't mind if they come and get them one right after the other. I'm ready. I don't like doing my work on the run. That's why I come early.

My pay is $320 a week; it is what all of us grooms make. When I first started at Arlington, it was $240. And I have an apartment (rent free). Gene Cilio made up the list of who was going to get an apartment (in one of the nearby buildings owned by Sportsman's Park) and who was going to get rooms (in the track dormitories), and Mauricio and I ended up on the list of apartments.

We get a reward when one of our horses wins. The owner gives me my stake — a bonus. When it is a small race, they give you fifty dollars. I haven't had many horses that run in big races. At Arlington, the mare (Sandy's Way) that broke my foot, she won two races. The owner of that mare, he gave me two-hundred dollars, and Gene Cilio also gave me two-hundred dollars.

What happens if I get sick? I am not very sickly…and my kids don't get sick, either. The only thing that happened was when my horse broke my foot. I had to go to the doctor, and my boss was the one who paid for all that. And I have (backstretch) insurance here.

The horse didn't kick me. She stepped on my foot. It was January 21st of last year (2000). There was a lot of snow on the roof of the barn, and water kept coming in and coming in. I was busy putting on the bandages when she got splashed in the face with some water. She got scared and turned around without giving me time to get out of her way. I was putting the bandage on her back leg when she turned and pulled and unhooked the chain and stepped on my foot and broke it. After that I couldn't work for two and a half months.

I couldn't walk. I was mad, and I got bored in my house. All I did was watch TV. I don't like wasting the whole day watching TV. I feel better when I am with my horses.

So that was a problem I did have for a while. But my life has mainly been peaceful with my horses. I feel proud to work with them. And as far as people problems go, I look at everybody as if they were my family. I am very comfortable here.

They have parties here in the grandstand, they give presents to the kids…everybody gets together. The trailer people (Illinois Thoroughbred Horsemen's Association, whose staff is housed in a backstretch trailer) give the parties. Every year the bosses give us sweatshirts. We have so many good things here.

I like to help people. A month ago I was coming out of my apartment early in the morning when I saw a girl who lives in the building. Her husband had gone to Louisiana, and she had stayed here with her husband's brother…her brother-in-law…and his wife, the three of them live in the apartment upstairs.

I asked her, "Are you already going to work?" And she put her hands on her stomach and said, "Ah, Maria…" I knew she was pregnant, and I asked her, "Are you going to the hospital?" She said, "Yes, Maria."

Then she turned around and almost fell and I grabbed her. Her brother-in-law was going to take her to the hospital. He was going to get the car when she was about to have her baby.

"Come on! Take her inside!" I shouted. And I put her in my apartment and put her in my bed, and I brought a chair next to the bed. They brought me a towel, and then and there she had the baby. I told her, "Don't be afraid."

When the ambulance came, the baby was already born…a big, strong baby. And that baby was born right in my apartment!

I like to help people. My life was very difficult…but I thank God I am here. After all I suffered, why should other people have to suffer?

CHAPTER 7

BARBARA D. LIVINGSTON

₱assionate Vision

Barbara Livingston was a teenager when she saved up her allowance and bought her first camera.

"My mom was divorced from my dad and had begun dating a man who did photography as a hobby. I think that she saw a chance for she and I to get closer through this camera, so she went with me to buy it."

The morning after her purchase Livingston went out and shot her first roll of film, snapping pictures of the sunrise. She promptly entered these shots in the Schenectady Gazette Photo Contest in her home state of New York and won first place. She pocketed the twenty-five dollars prize money and concluded: it can't get any better than this. It did.

Livingston has made a living out of doing what she loves most in the world: capturing images of racehorses. At age ten, she was horse crazy and could wrap a horse's leg perfectly. But by fifteen that was the last thing she wanted to do. "I just wanted to photograph them, touch them, see them, smell them, and capture them," she said.

Livingston still shoots rolls of film at sunrise and enters them in competitions. Today, though, these shots are featured in horse-racing publications, and have won her Thoroughbred racing's coveted Eclipse Award for outstanding photography.

Driven by an almost religious reverence for the horse, Livingston strives to capture its beauty for eternity. She is her own toughest critic; lessons in perfectionism were learned from a father who demanded excellence in all she did. For her, photographing horses is a mission. And she'll tell you, deadly serious, "There's nothing else I could do. I would just die."

I've often wondered where this strong connection I have to horses came from. I have no other passion in my life like it. I'd like to say men, or my husband, but that's not true because horses go far past that. I think it's because I trust horses where I don't always trust people. And horses have always been fair to me, and they're magical creatures. As Julie (Krone, the jockey and Livingston's longtime friend) said at the Hall of Fame induction ceremony last year, if she weren't a Christian she would worship horses. That's how I feel. I'm not a Christian. I almost do worship horses.

I've been injured by horses. I got a bad neck injury once. But that didn't alter my feelings about them. If anything, it was my fault for not paying attention. The horse gave me about a two-second warning, and I didn't heed it. After he threw me off, he stopped and came back and waited for me.

Barbara Livingston clicked with her first camera (right). With a favorite pensioner, Gato Del Sol (below.)

I've had relationships with people whom I've trusted totally, and they've taken all my money, my belongings, my car; they've taken my heart. I've never had a horse take anything from me that I didn't offer wholeheartedly. I definitely trust horses more than people. You can understand horses. Even a mean horse. If you watch him, you can understand why he's mean, and you can work with that. People, you just can't.

When I started college (at Syracuse University), I went for art and photography at first, but my artwork was just so awful that I changed the major to experimental photography. Occasionally I still do paintings and drawings, but not often. I'm just not as good at it as I want to be. There is a Sir Alfred Munnings exhibit at the Racing Museum that is extraordinary. His work makes me tearful to look at it. I would never be that good of a painter no matter how hard I try. But, to be honest, I don't feel the same way about photography as compared to painting. I've never found a photographer [whose work I couldn't rival] if I try hard enough.

When most artists do a painting, and it was true of me, it's almost impossible to get the looseness that can exist in a photograph. With Munnings, or Frederick Remington in his etchings from the late 1800s and early 1900s, they actually have the feel that they are still photos that just happened to be captured and put on canvas. But that is a rare gift, what those men had. I never found the looseness in my painting that I could with a photograph.

I have so many people say to me, "Well, you're a photographer, you're not an artist." That throws me. I'm as close to being an artist as I can. And there is a real difference between photographers. There are many successful photographers that can't see a mood shot. I can stand next to them for a week taking pictures, the same horses, the same setting. And theirs is going to look like a horse galloping; it's never going to have the same feeling as mine.

I always say that anyone can take a race win photo, which to some extent is not true, but really, almost anyone can at one five-hundredths of a second with a good camera. As long as a horse is somewhere near that finish wire, it's pretty darn easy.

But to actually get something where you can look into the soul of the animal, like you can almost feel it breathing or feel its veins popping out, watch the sweat streaming down it, that's something that not everybody can capture.

Whether one's better than the other is a whole different matter. But I want to make mine look like a painting. I want each horse captured for eternity in its most beautiful state.

You know, when I was a girl, I would read the books about Bucephalus and Alexander the Great and Pegasus. The true horses of imagination are horses that are beyond reality. And for me that was what I'd look up to and that's what every Thoroughbred that went by was. A part of Bucephalus was in this horse.

I grew up working around polo ponies, wishing they were racehorses. I made my folks start taking me to Saratoga by the time I was ten or eleven. I had such a love for it. I was reading horse books voraciously and admiring pictures of Man o' War. I drew pictures of him, based on photos I'd seen in books. Man o' War fascinated me. I started working summers when I was fourteen, pulling strawberries, and I would get a dollar each for walking the polo ponies at the matches and two dollars each for wrapping their legs after you walked them. When I was sixteen, I worked part-time at Kmart. All the money I earned I used to start buying books on the history of racing and photography books about horses.

And all of the sudden along came a horse named Secretariat and at the same time Riva Ridge. When Secretariat was three, I managed to get my family hooked enough for them to bring me out to the morning workouts. Secretariat broke two track records one morning in a workout in the slop when we were there. I was thirteen at the time. That was it for me. I just knew I wanted to be a photographer and work for *The Blood-Horse* and capture racehorses. I started working at the track as a hot walker. Then I started taking pictures there, and that took over, and I was set for life.

Everyone in my family has been very positive, and no one has ever tried to steer me in any other direction. My father really ingrained in us early that we had to make a living for ourselves. But I had a boyfriend that told me that I'd never be a famous photographer. That I was just going to be a housewife. I still want to show him. All these years later I still remember him looking me in the eyes and saying I wouldn't be famous.

When I started out, gender was a huge issue in my field of work.

When I was growing up and was friends with Julie back in the Dark Ages, she used to insist to people that it made no difference. And to some extent she still insists that. She still tells people, you know, "Don't think of me as a female jockey. I'm a jockey that happens to be female." But for me, I'll say flat out it made a huge difference. I think it made it much more difficult. I had a lot of trouble getting as much respect as the men that wore the big brown photo vests and carried Nikons and the various things.

A lot of photographers made my life very difficult when I came out. They would make up stories about me and tell clients terrible things about me, which were flat-out lies. Why did they do that? I always thought it was insecurity on their part, which is funny, because the two that I'm thinking of right now were both capable photographers. I found it very odd that they would waste their mental energy attacking me.

I got a lot of positive feedback on the Turnback the Alarm photo that wound up winning the Eclipse Award (1992). *(Editors' note: Livingston's photo captures Turnback the Alarm on her way to the racetrack and her image is reflected in a large puddle.)* After it was published, one of these men said to me, "It's a great shot." And I thought, "Wow, I've made it; this guy actually gave me a compliment!" Then, after I got the award months later, the same guy was standing with a group of people one day and he said, "Barb, you got to admit, anybody could have taken that shot that was there that day."

So, here it is twenty years later and they still do stuff like that on occasion. I think these guys are so hard on me because I'm just such a girl. You just see me walking around, and I'm smiling at everybody, feeding apples to the horses. Some of it is about competition — this is a very competitive business. There is something about me being a bubbly, happy girl that really annoys them. A lot of these people don't love the horses. I just *have* to do this work because I love horses. I can't do anything else. I walk into that paddock, and there's nowhere else I'd rather be.

I've been asked, "Is this a girl-horse kind of thing?" Well, how many men do you know that are truly sensitive? Every time a horse breaks down at that racetrack, you will find me out there crying, and I don't do it on purpose. I don't know if men are less sensitive, but for them it's just not socially acceptable. If a man cries when a horse breaks down, people are going to think, "Wow, what a girl." I think that's sort of built into it all.

I have a few things that I always have thought have helped me as a photographer. One, I worked with horses; I was galloping around on them long before I ever held a camera. So, when they tuck an ear back, or when I see them start to skitter out on the track, I can think what they're thinking, and I can probably know ahead of time what they're going to do. I think that's a huge advantage I have over a lot of other photographers.

Most of the photographers that are out there that I work with have very little patience. Their job is to get AN image, not *the* image. If a horse is standing there, *click*, they shoot it. I will wait and watch that horse in the walking ring for ten minutes to see if he just might do something — flick an ear, or look at a car going by, or something. Very often I don't get the image that I'm looking for. But I'll keep on looking for it.

Part of it is that I don't need to get a shot out to a daily paper at a quick turn around. I can actually try to get a beautiful portrait of a horse like Dream Supreme with (trainer) Bill Mott. Once the race is over, the other photographers are gone, and I'll be back there at the barn harassing Bill, "Can you please pose with this filly?" And he will; he could not be more gracious. So I can work to get something that's more historically relevant than what every track photographer or wire-service person can provide.

Another advantage I have, and this is an odd thing, is that when I was young I was cross-eyed. I had surgery when I was seven or eight. In fact, I had multiple surgeries. I lost vision in one eye. The other eye won out, and I basically have monocular vision, although I see colors with both eyes.

Anyway, because of this, I see the world at two-dimension. I've never seen anything in 3-D that I remember. So, everything I see is like a photograph. I happen to see like a camera sees. It wasn't long ago that I learned that Mr. Munnings was blind in his right eye and that he had monocular vision.

Everybody does think it's really wonderful and very easy to be a photographer. You'd be surprised how many people I meet who say, "I'm a photographer, too."

I have a friend who's a writer, and he said he has the same problem. "No you don't," I told him, because how many people actually go on vacation and bring their journals and start writing? But how many bring their cameras?

At the track while I'm working, I'll be bumping into all kinds of amateur photographers. I spend a lot of my time dealing with that and trying to help everybody, while behind me people are yelling at me, "Get out of my way; you're in the way of my shot." Sometimes I'll ask them, "What's your job?" And they say, "I work for, you know, a computer firm." And I say, "Well, how would you like if I just come and sit down in front of you at your computer, you know, just poke at it, while you're working?"

The reality is that we work incredibly hard because everybody wants to be us. Everybody thinks it's very easy, but we pay our own expenses, we pay for our own equipment. I'm there in the mornings just to get photos ready in case a publication calls me for them or an advertiser might need one. It's a hard way to make a living even when you're at the top of the game.

Last summer there was an owner that had a new stallion, and the new stallion had six or seven foals that he wanted to photograph together. They weren't yearlings yet, but he wanted the photograph without their mothers. So they insist it would be fine weaning them all at that moment. We were in the paddock, a very large paddock, and we weaned the six babies who noticed quite instantly that their mothers were missing. But worse yet, the mothers were in a paddock around ten yards away. So of course the babies started galloping around in circles. They were falling into feed tubs, they were…It was a melee, and the people were running around and screaming and trying to get the mares back out of the other paddock to bring them back. And three or four of them came running at me at dead speed. And boy, it sure was a beautiful image. And I shot a few frames and I realized that this dark face was getting really close, so I put down the camera and there he was. And he was so blinded with fear that he ran directly into me and knocked me down. Knocked me unconscious and broke a camera. I fractured my elbow. Somebody picked me up and carried me out of there, and I laid down for a few hours. It was over ninety degrees, and I went back out and finished the shoot.

I feel that I'm a very tight-knit member of the racing family. The grooms I'm especially nice to because I married one (Guy Jenkins) and I know what they go through. The exercise riders, that's a terribly dangerous job and it looks glorious and everybody wants to be an exercise rider, but boy, that's a tough job. So I try to at least know a little something about them, their families at home. And I think they know that I'm trying to capture the beauty of the horse. A lot of them, you know, will stand up straight or hold their horses a little more proudly. And I will absolutely give them a shot if they help me out with it, because for a groom, a picture of him with the horse, they'll keep it on their wall forever or send it to their parents in France or Puerto Rico. I love being able to do that when I can.

Things changed for me when I won the Eclipse Award, but that didn't make as much of a difference as I thought it would as far as name recognition. I still find major trainers who have no idea who I am even though I publish photos of their horse all the time. But it's improving. I'm a partner in a web site, and that's helped. And about five, six years ago people started calling me and saying, "We love your mood work. We've been noticing your mood work." That's all helped improve my business.

I get interested in certain horses. Artax (the 1999 Eclipse champion sprinter), I love shooting Artax. He's a very cool customer, very intelligent. I must have three thousand shots of him. He looks at you like a college professor looking at a student. He just views you and says, "you can watch me in my day, that'll be fine, and maybe you'll learn something." And he's also beautiful to look at, which certainly doesn't hurt, although I've photographed some horses — well, Skip Away wasn't the handsomest horse, but he had a very wise way to him.

Then there's Cigar. It's possible that I'll never find a better horse to photograph. I followed him through his last seventeen races. The first time I ever saw him he scared me, because he had such a white-rimmed eye, and he just gave me the creeps, and I didn't want to photograph him. But as time went on, I got to love that eye, and I got to thinking he wasn't really trying to give me the creeps. He was just sizing me up. It ended up being an amazing relationship I had with him. The pictures of him out on the track where he just looks like he could eat up the whole world…It'll be amazing if I ever find a better one than him while I'm alive.

One of the rewarding things for me lately has been when I have little girls ask for autographs and write to me and ask for a picture or an autograph. It's just such a kick for me, because that's what I used to do, although none of the photographers answered me back.

So, I answer every single request, and I send them a four-by-six and I autograph it. And when they write, "I want to be a horse photographer, too," — and I probably get ten e-mails a week that say that — I write back and say, "Never, ever give up no matter what, no matter who is mean to you. When you think you've taken a beautiful picture, show it to ten people, and they'll all tell you what's wrong with it. Learn that you're never perfect. Learn that you've got to keep trying to make yourself better."

When I did my college final in experimental photography, you could pick any subject you wanted. You could do anything, use any materials.

I did a series of self-portraits, which many people do. But throughout mine I interspersed pictures of Man o' War, Whirlaway, other horses from the past; very odd and surreal imagery. I used these photos only for my project — I could never commercially market anything like that. They weren't mine.

What I want is for people to have the same feeling toward my images that I had toward those great images taken by (L.S.)

Sutcliffe and Bert Clark Thayer and Allen Brewer — these people that came before me and who made me understand that Ribot breathed fire when he walked and that Man o' War held his head higher four days before he died than almost any horse here today ever would.

There are people who will never be able to see in person the memorable horses that I see. But I want them to be able to do that through my pictures — to bring to people what these horses feel like, look like, smell like, what they are. I want to be the conduit that connects them.

I want them to know Cigar had that creepy eye that just brought you in.

CHAPTER 8

M A R Y   S C O L L A Y

Speaking Their Language

Mary Scollay is one of the last lines of defense for bettors and their money. As a veterinarian for Gulfstream Park and Calder Race Course, Scollay is charged with making sure all entrants are "racing sound." In so doing, she ensures that healthy Thoroughbreds will carry fans' hopes and dollars. It is, as she puts it, "a major responsibility" that she takes very, very seriously.

Scollay was born in Birmingham, Alabama, in 1958. Not long thereafter, she and her family moved to Palatine, Illinois. Her father worked as an advertising executive in nearby Chicago. She grew up in Palatine and began riding as a youngster. Her interest in horses was one that, she said, her parents hoped she would outgrow. It didn't happen. When she was eleven, she found Majestic Prince's televised victories in the Kentucky Derby and Preakness to be electrifying: "I idolized Majestic Prince," she said.

After attending Augustana College in South Dakota, Scollay trans-

ferred to the University of Illinois, where she entered veterinary school. She graduated in 1984, worked four years in private veterinary practices, and then accepted a part-time post with the Illinois Racing Board. That led to her becoming a full-time association veterinarian at the Chicago Thoroughbred tracks. She assumed her current positions at the Florida tracks in 1995. Four years later she was honored in a public ceremony as Calder's Employee of the Year, the first member of her profession to earn that award. In 1999 she also served as racetrack veterinarian for Breeders' Cup XVI at Gulfstream Park.

Scollay and her husband, longtime jockey's valet Jim Ward, make their home in Fort Lauderdale, Florida.

M y going to vet school was actually kind of based on a family argument. The decision did not come to me in a dream or a vision. After high school I was all set to go to a women's college in Missouri, William Woods, that had an equestrian program. I was going to be an equestrianette. My dad got pretty mad at me. He said, "You know, you can't make a living doing that. And I'm not really looking forward to supporting you for the rest of my life. If you really want to work with animals, go to veterinary school."

I got a little mad at him. I said, "All right, but you're going to pay for it." He and I still laugh about that exchange.

It really wasn't something that I had thought about for a long time. I guess my interest was more obvious to other people than to

Mary Scollay's lifelong interest in animals led to her career as an equine veterinarian.

me. After we moved to Florida, I went back for a Palatine High School reunion. All these people there were showing each other photos of their children. But every time they'd see me, they'd whip out a picture of their dog or their cat, as if I could only relate to animals. They'd all assumed years before that I was going to be a vet. It never occurred to them that I was going to do anything else. It just struck me as very comical, that they thought I needed to see their dogs' pictures instead of their kids' pictures. It still strikes me that way.

I had started riding lessons when I was seven, much to the chagrin of my parents, who kept hoping I would outgrow this interest. I got my first horse when I was sixteen. He died three or four years ago. Lived to be thirty-four. His name was Airhead. He was a good friend. He's buried on the farm where I kept him, under a big tree. My husband and I have two horses here now, both retired racehorses.

When I was in veterinary school, there were quite a few women. We weren't fifty percent of the class, but close to it. The class that followed mine was the first class there that had more women than men. Women, I believe, predominate now. I was told that a recent U. of I. class was ninety percent women.

After I graduated, I went into a mixed-field practice. The owner of the practice had a lot of Saddlebred and show-horse clients and a few broodmares and a few riding horse clients. Then there were some changes in the practice, and I had to leave.

I wanted to stay in the Chicago area. I got my first racetrack job with the Illinois Racing Board at Balmoral Park one year when they had a three-day per week Thoroughbred meeting. I enjoyed it and have stayed on the racetrack ever since.

I'd like to think that I'm very sensitive to the animals and their needs. But I'd have to say that my husband communicates better with horses than I do. I'm envious of that. Jim's one of those people who can literally talk to animals. I have always wished I could do that, but it's not something I've been able to learn, and it is not a gift I was given. Horses know that they can trust me and that I respect them. I guess those are my strengths. Horses are very tolerant, forgiving creatures. I really feel that my life is richer for being around them.

I heard someone say once that people treat animals the way they treat other people, and animals treat people the way they treat other animals. So I try very hard to treat animals as animals. I respect their behavior patterns and their body language, recognizing their defenses — and what makes them defensive. I try to behave non-threateningly to them and yet at times show them that I am alpha, that they need to listen to me and respect me even though they don't know me, that we have no history together. There is a psychology game going on here.

Working around horses has taught me a lot. They are 1,200 pounds, and they can hurt you without even trying. So you learn to become very sensitive to their body language and what they are paying attention to.

I still do some small-animal relief work. I got this reputation for being good with bad animals, which is not necessarily a fun reputation to have because then you get booked for the big Rottweilers, the ones that come in snarling and growling. Yet I very rarely get bitten. I very rarely feel the need to muzzle an animal. If it's a dog you're dealing with, be a dog with him.

I wasn't really taught that in veterinary school. I've been fortunate to work with people who have those skills. Some of the vet technicians I've worked with in various practices — they're the ones that work with the animals on a different level. You know, the doctor comes, looks at the animal's mouth and eyes and ears, and chats up the owner; it's kind of bada bing, bada boom. Then it's the technician that has to go back and clean out the dog's ears. That's the tough part. Technicians are people who really learn how to "be" around animals. I've learned an awful lot from them.

When I worked in Chicago, I used to play this game in the paddock before a race. Steve Morgan, who was an assistant steward at the time, was in the paddock a lot as part of his job, and I was there as track vet.

Horses are very used to being sort of…well, dismissed. You know, somebody leads them in there, somebody slaps a saddle on them, and out they go to the racetrack. Nobody really interacts with them. It's as if they're a piece of furniture or something.

I would say to Steve, "Watch this. I can make this horse look at me without me moving." First time it happened, he said, "What are you talking about?" I said, "Just watch."

As the horses would go around the walking ring; I'd pick out one, and I'd concentrate and make eye contact with him. The horse would look at me like he's thinking, "Wow." The next time he'd be led around, he'd come looking for me. He'd start to walk past, he's being led in a circle, but he'd look back over his shoulder to see if I was still looking at him. This happened all the time. I'd made a connection with the horse without moving my arms or raising my voice — just with eye contact. Steve was really surprised. It makes me wonder what horses think of us.

It is things like that which have made me think about how to approach horses. As you walk into a stall, you can see how the horse feels about your presence there. Some don't care. Some of them are apprehensive. Depending on the response they give you to your presence, that helps you decide how to proceed with the examination. Some horses are like old friends. Others, you have to take a few minutes, take a few steps using non-threatening behavior to let them know that what's going to follow isn't something to worry about.

A lot has to do with how you approach them. I try to come in from an angle, toward the horse's shoulder. If I've got a hand extended, I keep it down low. I make eye contact with the horse. I try to make the first physical contact quieting and relaxing. So many people like to pat or smack horses. That is not normal horse behavior. Particularly to a young, green horse, that is very unsettling and disruptive.

If you watch mares with foals, or even older horses — I've seen this with the ones Jim and I keep — they groom each other constantly. There's a lot of sort of mini-massaging that goes on, and sweeping strokes. If you can sort of mimic that soothing behavior, they will be very compliant with something that they recognize is not normal behavior.

I have lots of opportunities to watch horses. You need to learn something every day or you're not doing your job, no matter what the job is. I have been very fortunate in that I've seen some wonderful racehorses and lots of not-so-wonderful racehorses. And I get to see lots of people interact with these horses.

I watch my husband around these horses. Jim knows when there is going to be a problem with a horse being saddled — usually before the trainer or the groom knows. He's that tuned in to their body language and the tension that he feels when he puts a hand on their shoulder, the stance they've got — all sorts of things.

Yet you can see somebody three stalls down who is absolutely oblivious to a horse that is about to explode. There are certain riders that can get on a very nervous horse, and that horse just settles down and relaxes. By the same token, you can see somebody who is very nervous and apprehensive on a horse who will get that horse to be just beside itself.

Then you've got them at the starting gate, where they are being put in a very unnatural situation. Horses are prey animals; they are meant to be somebody's dinners. When they can't flee something that's frightening them, they go crazy. And every time they race, we put them in this gate where they are very restricted, and then we clang this loud bell and send them on their way. Week after week we do this, and we expect them to just walk in like puppy dogs.

The starting gate is an area where you can see some really good horsemanship, or some really bad horsemanship. And you can see the effects of both.

There are certain trainers whose horses are almost always well behaved. There are other trainers who almost always seem to have troubled horses. There's a sort of trickle-down factor. A guy or a woman who is a good horseman has good help. They are going to insist on certain levels of behavior around their horses and certain levels of care. And that is reflected in the horses' behavior and attitude. There are trainers who are notorious for having bad gate horses. It's not the fault of the horse.

There's a question that I've wrestled with on more than one occasion: how I reconcile my love for horses with the fact that I am interacting with people who are not treating these horses in what is a really natural way. The first thing I understand is that these horse are professional athletes. They are not pets. And I am very careful not to get emotionally attached...I mean one of the ones we own now, French and Irish, I didn't own when he was a racehorse, but I was very emotionally attached to him, and I would worry terribly when he raced. I learned then that I could not own racehorses because of my personal attachment to them — my fear for their safety and the fact that I had no control once they were on the racetrack.

However, I will say that I have seen more cruelty at the hands of people who are alleged to love their pet horses than I have with people who have horses at the track. The racetrack is a business. You cannot expect your horse to provide you with his best performance, which is going to reward you financially, pay your bills, put food on your table, pay your mortgage, if he is not in good physical condition.

The negative feedback is instantaneous if they are not treated right. These horses, their intestinal tract, their musculo-skeletal system, everything says they are designed to be foragers. They should be out constantly ingesting small meals at frequent intervals. We all know this. So these racehorses get out of their stalls every day, their stalls are cleaned three or four times a day, they have fresh water, the best feed available, and they are monitored very closely.

I dealt with riding-horse situations at boarding facilities where horses would stand in their stalls from Monday through Friday, and then on Saturday and Sunday, pardon my French, they'd get the shit ridden out of them. Then they'd stand from Monday to Friday again. I have seen many more atrocities in the name of love than I have in the name of business.

This is not to say that I agree with everything that is done at the racetrack. My feeling about the racetrack is that by being there, maybe I can intervene and make a difference. I can't change the industry. But I can step up to the plate and say, "No, this is not acceptable. This cannot be."

I try to have a good working relationship with everybody. I don't like everybody, but I do my best to get along with everyone and be professional and pleasant. Because the day is going to come when there is going to be a confrontation. Sooner or later there will be a difference of opinion. That's just the way it goes. If I'm agreeing with everybody, I'm not doing my job. Hopefully I will have established enough of a background so that they will know, yes, she's a decent person, she's fair and objective. When the day comes that I have to say, "I don't agree with you on this," hopefully there's enough of a foundation there so that we can settle it in a professional manner and it doesn't turn into recriminations and biases and personality conflicts.

As far as my authority...well, I see horses that, if they were my own, they would not be racing. They've done enough, in my book. By the same token, I'm also aware that these horses are racing sound, and racing soundness is a large gray area. That's hard for a lot of people to understand. But when I'm looking at a five-year-old gelding that's a bottom claimer, and he's got big ankles, but he goes out and he runs and he comes back okay, as much as I would like to see him retired to my paddock, he can't come to my paddock.

And if I start to take stands based on my *personal* opinion, those horses are going to suffer more. They're going to go to the killers, or they'll wind up in somebody's livery string, or they're going to become a carthorse in Shipshewana. There's a large Amish community in Shipshewana, Indiana, and they buy a lot of horses off the racetrack at auction. It's not the kind of life you would wish for a racehorse.

There are times when a horse definitely has to leave the racetrack. "This is enough; we cannot go any further." But there are also times when you look at a horse and you say, "This old warrior is still here. He likes it. Let's not do him a disservice by making him not race anymore."

Maybe once a week I'll see a horse that does not belong out there on the racetrack. I'm fortunate in that at Calder we have a seven-month meet. So I get to know the population of horses and horsemen very well. Knowing the people is probably as important as knowing the horses. There are some trainers that I have known since I started on the racetrack, and they run a lot of horses, and I have never, ever put one of their horses in the horse ambulance. That's not to say that they run perfect horses. It is to say that they know their stock that well, and that for them my presence is superfluous. Which is what it should be. I'm the person that the racetrack [management] is delighted to pay to do nothing. They're glad to have nobody know that I'm there. If horsemen take care of their business, nobody has to deal with me.

On the other hand, there are people whom I deal with on a daily or weekly basis, telling them, "No, this isn't good enough." I go into the same barns and tell the same people, "The fly problem over here has got to be taken care of. Maybe we need to clean these stalls more often." You feel like a den mother. You feel like saying, "I shouldn't have to be telling you this."

The confrontational aspect of it is unpleasant. I used to find it very hard. At times it drives me nuts. But I've gotten meaner in my old age. And then sometimes something will jump up, and you will have made a difference, and you leave the other stuff behind.

We had a gate scratch a couple of weeks ago. Typically when that happens, the trainer (of the scratched horse) gets upset. I understand that. I mean, he led the horse over, he thought the horse was going to run, maybe the owner is there, and then he's publicly embarrassed because "on the advice of the track veterinarian, the number____ horse has been scratched" comes over the public address system. Everybody gets their hackles up a little bit when this happens to them.

But this guy a couple of weeks ago, he got real ignorant. He got really loud and abusive and rude to me. This is going on in the winner's circle at Gulfstream, and this trainer is just screaming at me. And I'm not in a position where I can get loud and abusive and rude back. All I can say is, "Sir, we have a difference of opinion, and in this situation my opinion prevails." You get mad, but you take it. The bottom line is that the horse is still scratched.

Two days later, another trainer came up to me and said, "We all heard what happened in the winner's circle. We all thought he was out of line for treating you like that. I just want you to know that we talked about it, and we are glad you are here looking out for our horses."

That's what helps you keep your perspective. That no matter what somebody says, you're looking out for the horses.

I think the majority of the people recognize the efforts that we take. We have a lot of problems with heat prostration in horses down here. People — the public — find that much more terrifying to see than a horse with a fractured leg. Maybe that's because they understand a fracture, but with heat prostration, horses get very violent and they fall down and then jump up; they're very erratic, almost like they're having a seizure. The public gets very worried about these horses.

And invariably, once we've gotten the horse straightened out and back on his way to the barn safely, and there'll be a couple hundred people in the area who have been watching, they will applaud. Or they will come up and say, "Good job, Doc." Patrons I don't even know.

I think that is something that the industry really needs to recognize — that the racing fan, which we desperately need, cares very much about the horse. We haven't yet as an industry figured out how to address the fact that these horses are professional athletes who do get hurt.

We had a horse a couple of years ago at Gulfstream, right in the stretch in front of everybody, that fractured its leg. It was apparent to me that it was a life-threatening injury. But this filly was by Seattle Slew out of a Secretariat mare, very well bred. The trainer came out on the track. I said, "This looks pretty bad." But we stabilized her and sent her off in the ambulance. They were going to try to save her.

During the following race, this mother came up to me with her young daughter. They both have tears in their eyes. The mother says to the daughter, "You ask her." And the girl says to me, "We were worried about that horse. They didn't tell us about the horse. How is the horse?"

I thought, how very brave of this little girl to come up to someone she doesn't know and ask that kind of question. It made me feel that we are not serving the public well enough in terms of being honest with them.

I don't know how this could be remedied. I've spoken to Vic Stauffer about it. He's our announcer. Part of the problem is that it is not something that can be done in a sound bite. You just can't say, "The horse fractured a leg and he may have to be destroyed." Because that doesn't help tell the story. People will go back to their old assumption that if a horse breaks its leg, it will be killed. Which is not always true.

Racetracks have fan education programs. They should be an opportunity seized by management to talk about what veterinary medicine is able to do for these horses. What the outcome of some of these situations are. That not all fractures mean a dead horse. And that career-ending injuries can result in a productive life afterwards. Not to sugarcoat the situation, but to give some information that is currently missing.

People will come up to me and say, "Doc, give me a winner." And I'll say to them, "Do you see me wearing new clothes every day? Do you see any jewelry on these fingers? If I knew something about how these races were going to come out, I would not be trudging back and forth to the paddock every day."

They'll say, "I guess you're right, Doc." And they'll be thinking to themselves, "Well, she's not too bright." Yes, the public perception is that there is a lot of "insider" information and that I know exactly what's going on.

The best story along those lines as far as I'm concerned happened at Arlington one year. There was a horse who flipped and got loose in the walking ring and ran around and did everything but turn inside out.

It just so happened that there was a guy there at Arlington that day who was my first boyfriend from high school, ever. I hadn't seen him since. They had been doing these patron information programs during the afternoon and my face had been up on that big television screen in the infield and he saw it.

So he came to the paddock, and he said, "Dr. Scollay?" And I said, "Yeahhh…" I'm thinking "Who is this? I don't know this guy; he's kind of chubby, balding." And he tells me his name, and I said, "No, you're not." So he pulls out his driver's license and proved to me who he was. The last time I'd seen him he'd been thin, and he looked like a rock star.

Anyway, he and his wife were there, and they were very nice; we were talking. Then I had to excuse myself because this horse had just gone berserk in the walking ring. I caught the horse and gave it back to the groom. So my old boyfriend says, "Help us out here. Give us a winner." And I said, "Well, I can tell you one horse not to bet," pointing to the one who had been acting berserk.

And, of course, that's the horse who won the race.

Dad used to take me to Arlington when I was little. They had a thing called the Railbird Club. Every Saturday morning we'd go out, and I'd collect horseshoes and other stuff. I saved a track program from one of those days in 1968. My parents found it when they moved out of their house in Palatine. I had put it under a carpet corner in my bedroom. Earlie Fires was riding then; Charlie Vinci was training — all these people that I'm working with today, that I see today. Earlie and (his wife) Kathy came to our wedding. It was like Pete Rose coming to a baseball fan's wedding.

(Former jockey) Bill Hartack, who was a steward in Chicago when I was working there, he rode Majestic Prince, who was my favorite horse of all time. When I had to go into the stewards' office that first summer I worked at Arlington, I couldn't even speak straight to him I was so nervous. I was just a blithering idiot.

Finally, after days went by, Bill took me out to dinner one night and told me racetrack stories, and I laughed until my face hurt. We've been friends ever since. Is that lucky? How many people actually get to meet and then know someone who had so much importance to them?

I would say that most days I love my work. I would imagine I'm like most people who have some days when they say, "This just isn't worth it." But I'm still a racing fan. I get paid every day to go to the races. How lucky is that?

CHAPTER 9

C H R I S T I N E   J A N K S

*T*he Nonconformist

G*rowing up the daughter of a wealthy industrialist in Lake Forest, Illinois, Christine Janks seemed an unlikely prospect as a successful trainer of Thoroughbreds and a prominent and forceful leader of horsemen's groups.*

But that was the path chosen by Janks, whose public stable is a major force at the Chicago Thoroughbred tracks.

After riding show horses as a youngster, Janks got hooked on racing during visits to Arlington Park with her father, Newton Korhumel, an enthusiastic fan and bettor. She started working there in 1967 at age seventeen as an exercise rider for trainer Pete DiVito. Shortly thereafter she got her own trainer's license (before she was even old enough to vote) and began conditioning a small string of horses owned by her father.

Janks' first important stakes winner was the fleet filly Cycyla Zee, heroine of the 1976 Arlington Matron and the Miss Tropical Park

Stakes at Calder Race Course the same year. She has tutored numerous stakes winners since then, including Shed Some Light, Blazed Star, Miwahiwa, and Playtime. In 1995 she became the first woman in Illinois racing history whose stable topped the million-dollar mark in earnings; her total of $1,176,770 placed her second in the national standings for female trainers. Janks finished second in the overall standings at the Hawthorne meeting that year and third at Sportsman's Park. She saddled more winners that season — seventy-one — than any other woman in the United States.

Christine Janks is a frequent presence in the winner's circle at Chicago-area tracks.

Janks has had other notable "firsts" as well, major among them her election as president of the Chicago division of the Horsemen's Benevolent and Protective Association in 1992, after which she became the first woman to serve on the association's national board. In 1995, when the Chicago division folded, Janks was elected president of its successor, the Illinois Thoroughbred Horsemen's Association, a post from which she retired in 1997.

In addition to her on-track responsibilities, Janks and her husband, Barry, own and operate Emerald Ridge Farm near Mundelein, Illinois, and Carson's Springs Farm near Gainesville, Florida.

I have always had this nonconformist thing. Even when I got sent away to boarding school when I was sixteen...I was really very unhappy there. So I dyed my hair bright pink, and I swallowed goldfish for a dollar apiece. I was constantly doing stuff like that. It was always an adventure to sort of outwit the opposition, which at that point was usually the school, my teachers. Art and carpentry — it was called "shop" at Country Day School — and creative writing were my three A's. The rest of my grades were pretty grim.

It finally got so bad that the headmaster, who really liked me, said, "Look, if you keep this up I'm going to have to throw you out, and I really don't want to do that. Because even though your grades aren't very good, and I let you in here with grades that weren't what we usually accept, you were just a unique personality that I enjoy. But you've just got to cut this stuff out, or I am going to have to throw you out." My parents called me and said, "If you don't get thrown out, we'll let you go to school at home next year. But just don't get expelled." So I made it through the year there at Garrison Forest. It's in Maryland, near Towson.

I can fondly say of my dad that he is a control freak, and I really have to tone down my tendency to try and control everything and go against the grain. I said to my mother not long ago, "If you

Janks' father supported her in all her equine endeavors.

only had used reverse psychology with me when I was a kid, you would have gotten much more satisfaction out of me." Because no matter what it was she said, I was bound and determined to go forth and do the opposite. I really take after my dad. I have to say that I have always had a close relationship with him. In the last couple of years, I have gotten a lot closer to my mother. We have had a learning experience about each other that has been sort of a revelation to both of us.

I grew up in Lake Forest in a very wealthy neighborhood. We were well-to-do. It was Cotillion, Junior League, prep school, Ivy League colleges, that was where I was expected to head.

I was just obsessed with horses from the time I was five years old. We had forty acres on our place and a barn. Every girl in my class at school loved horses, and we all did riding, but very few of them stuck with it.

So, I just really wanted to get into the horse thing, and I used to come to the races with my dad. He was a very good handicapper. He liked to come to the track and gamble. My dad was always the ultimate family man, because, for instance, every night he would be home for dinner at 6:15, and we sat the whole family — I have two brothers — down to dinner at 6:30 every night. On weekends we did things together.

But the other side of it was he would go to Vegas and gamble, and he was game to try anything. My dad is ninety-five now and still going strong. I'll never forget, when he was in his fifties, we went to Aspen. He had never skied in his life. We were all on skis at the top of the mountain, going down in a wild heap, the whole family. We did things as a family. He had a very adventurous spirit, but he really promoted keeping the family together.

He is the most determined person I have ever seen to keep going, to refuse to concede anything to his age. He was in the steel business, and he still is in the steel business. He still has four companies. We are trying to get him to cut back some. He always had a very powerful work ethic. He went to Europe for Eisenhower after World War II to rebuild the steel mills and met with Churchill and did really interesting things.

My dad had a box at Arlington, and I would go with him, and it was sort of a father-daughter outing. This was in the late fifties. I was just a little kid, and I'd go down to the paddock and pick out the horses to bet. Dad would give me money to bet. I never bet now, but I used to bet then.

I got to the point where I didn't want him to make my bets for me, so I'd get in the [mutuel] line, and I'd get about two people back from the teller, and I'd say to the person in front of me, "Would you bet two dollars on the eight for me?" or whatever the number. The funny part of it was, if it was a woman I'd ask, for the most part they'd say, "You shouldn't be betting, little girl." If it was a man, he'd go, "Sure, honey." So I quickly learned who to ask. That was a big thrill for me — making my own bets. I've always been really competitive, so if my horse would win and my dad had bet a different horse, well, that was the ultimate thing.

I was involved in show horses for a long time. My dad even bought a riding stable to sort of support my interest, though it was also a real estate investment. [Showing horses] was fine, except at the horse shows it was always someone's opinion whether you won or not. That's what I love about the racetrack — it doesn't matter what color you are, what sex you are; all that mattered was who won. If you got there first, that was all that counted. There were obstacles, but the reality of it was answering the question of who got there first.

Plus, there was the business element. I mean, there is big money involved. If you are going to be successful, you can't ignore that part of it. That appealed to me as much as the horses. My father was the ultimate businessman, so maybe I took after him with my interest in the business side of it.

Someone brought some horses from the racetrack to board at our riding stable, and I got the idea that I could go out and gallop at the track. I came out to Arlington one summer to do that and got on horses for Pete DiVito. There were no other women galloping horses there at the time.

I was seventeen. Of course, in the beginning I lied about my age. I started galloping, and I looked around and said, "This is the greatest thing I've ever seen in my life!" Number one, I was at that age where there were all these good-looking guys out there and no women — how come no one had discovered this? And I was making real money, my own money. I said, "This is for me. Who wants to get dressed up and go to dances or school?"

My dad was supportive. That first year we had a horse at the riding stable that was a former racehorse. I got the idea that I could make him back into a racehorse. At this point I was galloping horses for (trainer) Don Gibbons, and he said, "Why don't you take out a trainer's license?" And I thought, "Why not?" So I studied for my test and passed it with flying colors. I don't know if they gave me an easier test or what, but it was really simple. I mean for someone who had been around horses all their lives, it was very simple.

After it became obvious that the horse I brought back from the stable wasn't going to work out, my dad claimed a horse for me to train. As I said, he was very supportive. The first horse he claimed, the first time we ran it back it won. We were cheering. It was such a great thing. Then he claimed a couple more.

So, I put in for stalls at Gulfstream that winter. I went down there with the intent of training a few horses and also being a pony girl. I was going to pony horses to make a living. This was, like, my first venture on my own. I was eighteen. A couple of my horses got claimed, and my pony got hurt, and one thing led to another. So I came back to Chicago and I picked up a few horses at a sale, and I started back at Sportsman's Park at the end of April.

One of the first things I learned there was that there were no ladies' bathrooms on the backstretch — they didn't exist. You had to either go up to the grandstand or the racing office or something.

The men thought nothing of urinating on the trees on the backside or next to their cars or anywhere else, because there really weren't even any women as grooms or hot walkers. It was like one giant men's locker room.

I was such a novelty that, you know, guys were flirting with me — or else they were not taking me seriously. But to my advantage, if I needed stalls or if I needed something from the racing secretary, if I went in and sat down in his office and looked like I wasn't leaving until I got what I wanted, well, they didn't know what do with that. If it was a man, they'd just say "get the hell out of here." With me, the easiest thing for them to do was just to give me what I wanted.

Of course, there were disadvantages, too. It was hard to get clients. At that time most of the owners were men. There are maybe 250 men trainers (in Chicago). What wife is not going to say to her owner-husband, "Why do you have the only woman training for you?" And I can understand that. It was very helpful to me that my dad bought some horses so that I could prove I could train. I also picked up a few through the riding-stable connection, because those people were used to women being the primary person in charge of the horse. But I can remember men walking up and looking to be hired as grooms. They would come up to me and say, "Where is the trainer?" I'd say, "I am," and they would just give me this look and go, "I'm not working for no woman," and they'd walk away.

I'd just look at them and laugh, because there was always some-body else to hire. I had a lot of Spanish help; there are quite a few

Mexicans and other Spanish people in the Chicago area. The first couple of years I trained in Florida, they'd say "that's the girl that has all the Spanish help." It was kind of unusual then. But they were great with the horses. They liked the horses and they took a big interest in their jobs. That sort of carried through my whole career — my help has always been basically Spanish.

I remember my first groom. I was lucky to get that guy. He was an Argentine man who was just very, very good. I didn't know how to put a tongue-tie on a horse. So I'd say to him, "Luis, put a tongue-tie on that horse," and I would watch him do it. Then I'd go back to the riding stable, and I'd practice all afternoon and the next day I could do it, too.

Another day, I'd tell Luis to "put some run-downs (bandages) on," and I'd watch him do it. Then I'd go home and practice and practice until I could make them look just like he could make them look.

Basically, this really excellent groom taught me a lot of stuff. I tried to watch what everybody did. I am a big believer in common sense. That takes you a long way in the world. I made a lot of mistakes, and there were a lot of things I didn't know about training at first. But I have a really good feel for horses, and I think the details sort of all fell into place.

I don't speak much Spanish, just a little bit I learned from my first husband, Hector Viera, who I met and married quite quickly. He was a Cuban, and he was a jockey, and that did send my parents around the bend!

We told my parents, "We are going to get married in two weeks and we would like you to come." My dad blew his top. Like I said, he has always been very controlling, and it usually works in our family. He jumps up and starts screaming and hollering, and he said, "This isn't going to happen, you're not going to do this, you'll never come back into this house again." This was the first time he'd gotten quite that excited. But it just made me more determined.

So Hector and I got married that fall and that presented a whole new set of problems regarding the women in racing thing. At that time the rules all stated — there was a clause in the rules — that one ruling that applied to the husband shall also apply to the wife. So the first time Hector got a five-day suspension for rough riding or whatever it was, careless riding, they told me that I couldn't train any horses for five days.

It was like ridiculous! One day I'm at my barn and security guards come to escort me off the grounds. They said, "You can't be on the grounds because your husband is ruled off." I said, "But he can be on the grounds" — to work horses, even if he couldn't ride for five days. And they said, "Well, if you had some kind of medication ruling against you, he wouldn't be able to ride during that period of time."

So for a while we put the horses in my assistant trainer's name, my husband's uncle. They raced in his name because we were afraid that something inadvertent would happen and then how do you tell your owners? They (racing officials) told me, "You can't put the horses in your assistant's name for just five days; you've got to leave them in his name for the whole meeting, otherwise you are circumventing the rules."

I go, "The rule wasn't for me. I didn't do anything wrong." It was like they couldn't get it through their heads. It wasn't until quite some time after that — after somebody filed a lawsuit — that those rules were finally changed.

Another thing then — after we got married, it was perceived that Hector was really training the horses. He wasn't, but the perception was that I was just fronting for him.

It was kind of interesting to me then that being a jockey he had quite a bit of money. He was doing well with his career, and he bought a brand new car. We loaded it up, and when we drove through Tennessee — it's a new Cadillac and the back is full of stuff — the cops pull us over. They thought we'd stolen the car. I'm from Lake Forest — this is all new to me. Really exciting, but new! We showed the cop the registration. He was so disappointed that we actually owned the car and could prove it.

Hector and I had a very good marriage for a long, long time. And we are still very good friends. We just…it just faded out as far as the marriage part of it. But I think we still have a bond and he is a friend. I would help him and he would help me. He's in Florida now. He's training down there.

I always wanted to marry someone or be involved with someone that I could be with a lot of the time. It's like that now with my husband, Barry. People say to me, "How can you stand to work together all the time?" It's like we wouldn't have it any other way. Barry runs the farm here (in Illinois) and the farm down in Florida and is equally important to the whole process. He doesn't get the recognition and the attention because he is sort of behind the scenes. But, nonetheless, he's critically important.

That deal with the cop and the car in Tennessee was what you could call "ethnic profiling," I guess. Some of my friends have encountered similar situations with racism, other things like that. That kind of prejudice is out there. You just have to ignore it, because if you get angry, the only person it is holding back is you. I have said to people — whether they were women or black or Spanish — that you are going to run into people that are bigoted or racist or whatever. You've just got to go around them and keep on going because you can't let it alter your focus.

I think problems that women trainers have today lie in themselves. A lot of women don't succeed because of the way they conducted their business. They weren't competing in the same way as a man competes, and they focused on the wrong things.

One day at Sportsman's these two women trainers came up to me and they said, "Look at the [track] program. Do you see what they do here? For the men, they use initials like for J.R. Smith. But for women, they spell your name out. You know why? Because they want the bettors to know it's a woman trainer's horse, like maybe it is less well trained."

I said to them, "That's like looking at the cup being half full. I'm proud that I'm a woman, and I want my name in there."

Well, the way they were looking at it was that "someone's out to get us, they're trying to keep us down." And that limited them. And those women are not training horses any more.

It was like somebody said to me — one of my owners said to me the other day, "Oh, you're the leading woman trainer here." I said, "I'm just a trainer." I just try to have the fact that I am a woman not be an issue. Because if you allow people to make it one, it will persist. So many women allowed that to happen.

With women riders, it's interesting that when they first come to town they always come to my barn. I tell them right off, "I won't ride you because you are a woman, and I won't not ride you because you are a woman. You are just going to have to do it like everybody else."

I honestly don't think a lot of women, for purely physical reasons, have what it takes to be top jockeys. But when they first started riding, it just drove me nuts that they allowed themselves to be called jockettes. I used to tell them, "Don't let them do that. They don't call me a trainerette. They don't call them lawyerettes or doctorettes. Don't let them do that. You are a jockey like every other jockey."

I think I am much better now communicating with women than I used to be, but women are different now. So maybe that's it. My three really close girlfriends, none of them have had children and all of them have been really successful in business. I don't think it was an accident. I think you gravitate toward people like yourself. I never had any good girlfriends when I started in racing, because the women around were wives with kids. They just had different lives. As a result, I ended up hanging out with the men most of the time because what they were talking about was what I was interested in.

When I was president of the horsemen, people liked me because I wasn't afraid to stand up and charge forward. They didn't charge behind me, though; they just kind of pointed in the direction I should go. One day Diana Holland, who is the wife of one of the owners, she got up and said, "All you trainers are the same," but she was talking to the men, "all you want to do is hide behind her skirts." It was a great line.

One of the things I love in the world is being right. And when you get a horse and you train him for a race and you know the horse is doing good and you pick the spot that you think you can win, and then the horse wins, that's like the ultimate right. Because everybody entering that race thinks they can win and expects to win. Only one person is really right. You build up and put this whole thing together…it's the ultimate right.

The ugly side of the business is that a lot of the horses come to a bad end and that bothers me. A lot of them come to a bad end due to the fact that there are trainers that shouldn't have licenses because they have no feelings for the horse. It's a business, yes, but we're dealing with a living, breathing, pain-feeling animal. That part gets lost too much.

Yes, I think you can get too attached to horses. I don't mean to take anything away, but the reality is that people get in car accidents, people step off curbs and break their legs. I mean things happen. But the fact that some of the really good horses end up running in cheaper and cheaper claimers until they finally end up in a heap on the track really makes me sick. I don't know what the answer is, because people are cruel to dogs, they are cruel to cats, sometimes they are cruel to their children.

I've had many horses break down, and we have saved many horses. I have a mare by the name of Catching a Buzz that broke down horribly when she was actually pregnant carrying her first foal. She had just won two races in a row. In the third race her sesamoid snapped, and the jockey, Francisco Torres, just did a tremendous job of saving her by keeping her from falling. It just made me so sad.

But Charlie Burton, who worked for me at the time, did a tremendous job of changing the bandages and taking care of her for months. And Catching a Buzz has been our broodmare for ten years, and she is the mother of a stakes winner. That was a good end.

I am in sort of a transitional period now. I would like to cut back on my training a lot and upgrade some of my horses. I would also like to spend more time at the farm. I am interested in the garden, and I love to read. I have no idea if I could, but I feel like I could write fiction, not necessarily about the racetrack.

I have always said to people that if racing ended tomorrow that

I would be fine. There are lots of other things that I could do. There are so many things that I would have liked to have done in my life, different jobs, different careers. This business can be so emotionally draining.

The parts that I love best? In the afternoons, I love running my own horses. But I am never at the races if I don't have a horse running. I don't gamble, and I'm not claiming horses, so I won't be there unless I'm running something.

Some mornings I'll pull up in the truck (at the track) and I'll have the radio on and the sun is coming up, and, oh my God, it just gives me goose bumps. The horses are galloping along and snorting, they're in rhythm…

It is such an emotional thing, such an enveloping experience. I think that's what you feel. When you come out here, it's not like you watch a football game — to me, that's out there, removed — but here it's a surrounding experience. When you are here, it sort of envelops you.

J A N E   G O L D S T E I N

$\mathcal{P}$remier Publicist

Racing writer JoAnne Stover once said that with Jane Goldstein's *"collected look and conservative appearance, she looks like she should be running an art gallery in San Francisco or a bookstore in Brentwood instead of patrolling the Santa Anita backstretch in search of stories."*

Appearances can be misleading, as Stover went on to make clear. Goldstein may not have looked the part of a premier Thoroughbred racing publicist, but she served in that role for more than three decades.

A native of New Orleans, Goldstein was raised in the Crescent City, where her father was a newspaper man. After earning a bachelor's degree in journalism from Louisiana State University in 1960, she got a job as a publicist at the Fair Grounds. Subsequent publicity jobs followed at tracks all over the nation: Laurel Race Course, Pimlico, Hialeah, Keeneland, Churchill Downs, and Santa Anita.

Accepting a full-time, year-round job at Santa Anita enabled

Goldstein to end her nomadic yearly schedule that required her to move from track to track and city to city. She signed on with the Southern California track in 1975. Less than a year later she was named director of publicity — the first woman to hold such a post not only in Thoroughbred racing but in any major sport. In 1991 she was named to the track's newly created position of director of communications while continuing to head the publicity department.

A widely published free-lance writer, Goldstein's work appeared in such publications as The Blood-Horse, The Horsemen's Journal, *and* The Thoroughbred Record. *She has served as the American representative of the International Racing Bureau and director of publicity for the Colonial Cup International Steeplechase. She currently lives in Sierra Madre, California.*

I wanted to be a journalist, but I ended up in publicity. It was easier for some reason to get in on publicity staffs. And my philosophy was that I always felt I could make it in the working world. It wasn't that I was a woman trying to pioneer something. It was Jane trying to pioneer Jane.

I was painfully shy as a child. I was an only child. As I grew up, I got out of it, somewhat. But I wasn't going to the racetrack and going up to people and saying, "Hi, I'm Jane, and I want to meet you." I was really quite retiring. I think what helped me a lot was that being a journalist, or a publicist, I had a legitimate reason to meet people. That gave me some backbone. I just wanted it so badly

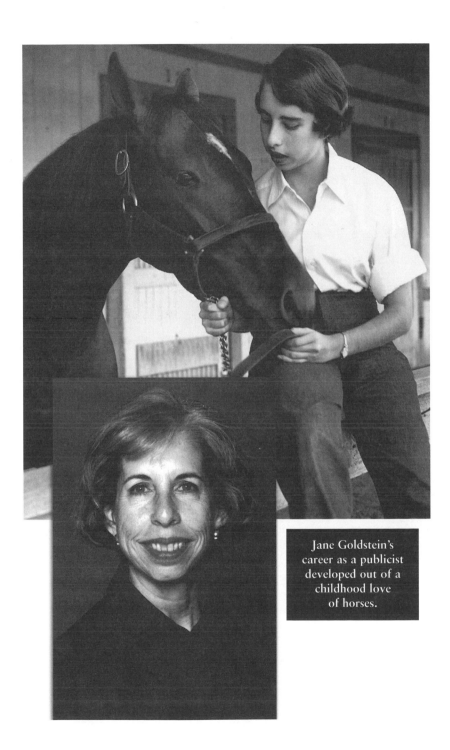

Jane Goldstein's career as a publicist developed out of a childhood love of horses.

that I made myself do it, even though the butterflies in the stomach could be intense most of the time. But if I wasn't going to be just a bystander looking in, I had to find a way to get into it myself.

All the uprising of women for equal rights in the workplace and so forth came after I was already working in racing. So I didn't jump on that bandwagon. I didn't feel any need to. I was already there.

It's true I was the first woman to head a publicity department. But I wasn't the first woman to work in that field in racing.

When I got started, it was hard. I'm sure I was terrified for the whole first five years. My picture of the backstretch then was very few women. The women who were there were working with the horses. In those days, I'm sure I wore a skirt, but I was an exception. The women who worked physically with the horses would have on jeans. So I knew I was sticking out and people were looking at me oddly. But I just kept on going. The old-time horsemen were gentlemen. Nobody was ever rude to me. I got along just fine. I think that today people on the backstretch aren't going to pay any attention to your sex; they're going to be rude to you if they want to be rude to you whether you're a male or a female.

My career developed out of a childhood love of horses, like so many young girls. When I was little, I collected figurines and pictures and books of horses. But my only involvement with them was that I would ask for money for my birthday or Christmas and save it up and take riding lessons at the riding academy in Audubon Park in New Orleans, where I grew up.

My father was a newspaper man. He was with the New Orleans *Times-Picayune* for many years. He was a general reporter for a while, and he did all kinds of features and interviews with celebrities who would come to town.

He had also been a book critic. He and some contemporaries of his had started a literary magazine in New Orleans called *The Double Dealer*. It was a very famous literary effort in the 1920s. They did the first, or the early, publication of a lot of people, including Ernest Hemingway and William Faulkner. I could say that my father had a lot to do with my love of writing and of literature.

My father liked to play the horses in a very, very small way. When the Fair Grounds was open, he usually had a weekday off, and he would go out and bet two dollars here and two dollars there.

So when I became interested in horses, one day he said, "I'll take you to the racetrack." And that just opened up a whole new world for me. I began buying whatever I could find to learn about racing. I was about eleven at the time. I found a magazine called *Turf & Sport Digest*, which was edited by a man named Raleigh Burroughs, who I met years later and who turned out to be a great guy. It was both a handicappers' magazine and a features magazine. Of course, I was interested in the features.

Then I discovered things like the *American Racing Manual*, and I would read it from front to back. None of my good friends were particularly interested in any of this. Basically, I was on my own with this interest. As I said, I was in the era when there were very few females working at the racetrack. I really never realistically had any idea of becoming even an exercise rider.

The attraction for me was the beauty of horses, the relationship you can have with them through riding. I can't explain it to you. And although I still admire horses, I must say that my young love of them wore off as I got away from the physical side of it. Later on, even though I was at the racetrack and seeing horses all the time, I was rarely involved with them hands on. Oh, once in a great while I'd get up on somebody's stable pony. But it scared me — not in the sense that it could be dangerous to me so much as I might do harm to somebody or somebody's good racehorse.

My first year of college, I went off to the University of Kentucky because I wanted to be around horses. But during my first year there my father became quite ill, so it just seemed more practical for me to go back to Louisiana and be closer to home. So I went to LSU in Baton Rouge and graduated from there.

When I was in high school, I wrote for the school newspaper. In college I sold a couple of articles to the *Times-Picayune* on racing subjects. The writing came very easily to me. Once I got sitting down at a typewriter then, or at a computer now, once I get a few words down it just sort of flows. It was always fun for me putting stories together. I think I was a junior in college when I realized I wanted to combine these two things, journalism and horse racing.

My father helped me a lot. He taught me to be concise, and he taught me the principles of a good journalistic story. My approach to publicity when I got into it was always to try to be a good journalist with your publicity materials because that way they'd be much more likely to be picked up and used.

I'd have to credit my father for his connections in getting me my first job. He knew Gar Moore, who was the general manager at the Fair Grounds. He called him up, and Gar Moore said, "Okay, we'll try her for a while." That was in 1961.

The Fair Grounds publicity staff at the time was pretty small. They worked out of the press box. The [Daily] Racing Form crew there were very nice to me. I guess they thought, "This is quite a kick," because a woman working there in the press box was unheard of.

There was a really tough sports editor of the Times-Picayune named Bill Keefe who used to go to the races almost every day. And there were going to be no women in the press box as long as he was there.

Keefe didn't get there until the afternoon, so I could work in the press box in the morning. Then I had to go somewhere else. Sometimes I'd just find a seat in the general offices.

Years later I applied to work in publicity at Monmouth [Park], and the general manager told me that he wanted to hire me. But there was an old curmudgeonly journalist there who wouldn't let women in the press box. So I didn't get hired at Monmouth until that guy retired.

In between, I moved to New York City and got a job. All that while, I was trying to get into racing. I went to the New York Racing

Association, to Delaware Park, Garden State…nothing worked.

I remember that I made an appointment to see the editor of *The Morning Telegraph* (at that time the sister paper of *Daily Racing Form*). He was very gracious, and he encouraged me to keep trying and so forth. He said, "But you know, we never have women working at the *Racing Form*." He told me that was the company policy.

However, I'd say within six months or so they hired a woman to write a column for the *Racing Form*. Her name was Patrice Jacobs; she was the daughter of one of the most prominent trainers in the country (Hirsch Jacobs), and today, of course, she is Patrice Wolfson (who co-owned 1978 Triple Crown winner Affirmed with her husband, Lou Wolfson). But it wasn't lost on me that the *Racing Form* policy changed abruptly for her. I certainly made note of that. I was disappointed.

But I didn't think it was the end of the world. I just thought, the *Racing Form* editor is just one guy. I can break into this sport another way. So I kept trying. Finally, I got hired at Laurel. I'd say that was my first real, full-time publicity job, and things just kept going from there. I just enjoyed being at the racetrack so much that I was determined to work there.

When I later finally got work in publicity, first at Laurel and then Pimlico and Monmouth, I felt most of the racing journalists were very welcoming. Walter Haight from the *Washington Post*, he was a lovely man. Dale Austin of the [Baltimore] *Sun*, Bill Boniface —

they never made me feel out of place. I think they thought I was kind of amusing. They would figuratively pat me on the head, that sort of thing.

I moved around a lot for years. I lived out of the trunk of my car. Whenever I bought a car, the first thing I looked at was how big the trunk was. I had clothes, some basic dishes and kitchen tools, and a typewriter.

In the end, I got to the point where I disliked all the moving. But not at first — at first, I got to see all kinds of parts of this country that I otherwise wouldn't have seen. I just loved living in various states and seeing what was there. I was a great explorer. I liked to visit both the cities and the countryside.

But it was hard, too. I was pretty much on my own. So when I got the chance to base myself in California, I finally took it. I'd been going from track to track for about fifteen years. It got to the point where I was at an age that I needed to settle down. Dan Smith helped me. Joe Burnham, Alan Balch, they all put in good words for me at Santa Anita.

When I was first named publicity director, I had some rough times. I had to battle with some of the newspaper guys from time to time. You get a bunch of handicappers and reporters in a press box, and they're not all going to want the same thing at the same time. I can remember one or two who tried to take advantage of my newness on the job. They just tried to bully me.

Some of the press-box guys wanted anybody and everybody to

be allowed in. Others wanted nobody but the working press up there. You try to be a diplomat. But I also tried to make it into more a working atmosphere than a play atmosphere.

There was many, many a day that I was sort of boiling inside, and hurt, but I tried to put on a good front. I tried to be a very professional person. You get into a lot more managerial, administrative kinds of stuff, workplace politics...there were many times when I thought, "I don't really like this job." I wasn't getting out as much on the backstretch with the horses and horsemen. I missed that.

From the start, looking for stories on the backstretch, I realized that these trainers, you know, they have a business to run. It's as if you're going straight into their offices when you go to their barns. I've always felt that you had to tread lightly when you went into a barn, because usually it was without an appointment, and it's like walking into a company president's private office. You can't run over them. When I had a staff under me years later, I would always tell them that. I would always tell journalists who weren't familiar with the racetrack to be considerate.

I'm inclined to think that there were more characters and more colorful people in racing years ago. But that could just be the time perspective. And maybe the journalists aren't trying to uncover stories that are lively and fun. Nowadays, the coverage of racing is so slanted toward business, business, business, and, in some cases, scandal.

Of course, the publicist working for the racetrack wants to put forth positive stuff. Her job is not to uncover dirt. It's to generate some news. I got to the point where I realized it's not our job to reveal bad news. But you can't cover it up, either. You have to be honest.

I have long wished that the journalists would do more of their own work — weren't as dependent on the publicity department. But that works both ways, because it is an advantage to the publicity people.

I took early retirement from Santa Anita on November 1, 1998. There were changes of ownership of the track, in the administration. For the previous two years, I had been fairly miserable. I started to feel that people didn't love horses as much as I did. And I finally decided, "I'm going to get out before they get me out. I'm going to do it on my own terms." And I did. And it worked out beautifully. I still do some work for them on a free-lance, a contract basis. So I'm still involved, but I don't have to go in every day.

Santa Anita's still my favorite track — for pure beauty, you can't beat it. Over the years I was lucky enough to be around great horses: Kelso, Forego, John Henry. Oh, I loved John Henry. And I knew great horsemen like Eddie Neloy and Allen Jerkens and Buddy Raines and Charlie Whittingham.

Charlie wasn't a great on-screen personality like some trainers today. He was quiet. He'd say things occasionally, but you'd almost have to pull them out of him. But you can't beat Whittingham for horsemanship, and he was an awfully nice fellow on top of it.

I think I achieved something both for myself and probably for women in general. And I got some attention because I was a woman working in the publicity field. I don't mean overwhelming attention, but every once in a while somebody wanted to do a story on me. I was well aware that what I was doing was unusual and that I had done well.

I have good friends in all aspects of racing, many of them female. I don't know a lot of women publicists. But there are some, and when I do run across them, I guess I'm thinking, "good for you."

CHAPTER 11

CHRISTINE SALVINO

The Soprano in the Paddock

First-time visitors to the paddock at two Chicago-area tracks have been somewhat startled in recent years to hear the traditional command of "riders up"— which alerts jockeys that it is time to get aboard their horses — delivered in a feminine tone.

Giving that order at Sportsman's Park and Hawthorne Race Course since 1987 has been Christine Salvino. She and Allison DeLuca, who later became a racing secretary and is now an official at Kentucky tracks, are believed to be the only two women ever to serve as paddock judges at racetracks in this country.

Salvino's road to a career with racehorses was a straight shot: She was born and raised in Cicero, Illinois, site of Sportsman's Park and neighbor of Hawthorne. She began working on the backstretch as a teenager. At twenty-one, she married fellow Cicero native Owen Salvino, and, thus, became part of a family heavily involved in Thoroughbred racing.

Owen Salvino's father, Ralph Salvino Sr., trained for nearly seven decades before his death at age eighty-six in 1995 (he still had a horse in training at the time). Ralph and his wife, Estelle, had eight sons including Owen (there were four daughters as well), and six have held trainer's licenses over the years. One son was a jockey, as were a grandson and a granddaughter. Other members of the Salvino clan have worked as clockers, exercise riders, and in clerical positions at Chicago tracks.

As far as I know, mine is the only female voice to be yelling out, "Riders up." It's funny when you have people come in from out of town for stakes races and they don't know me or about me. They'll hear me announce, "Riders up," and they'll look over at me like, "Are you kidding? What's going on here?"

When I started this job, I was scared to death. My entire training came on my first day when the man I succeeded, Vince Amato, met me in the paddock and said, "Okay, you're here." Then he went upstairs — he'd asked to be transferred and made a placing judge.

I basically knew from being around the track what the job entailed. But I was still terrified to say "riders up" the first time. There's no microphone. You just shout it out. I take a deep breath and let go. I stand pretty much around horses number one, two, and three, because if everybody sees those jockeys getting on, even if they can't hear me all the way down the line, they'll still know it's time. And everybody's anticipating it. After I've called the horses

Christine Salvino
gives the order
"Riders up" at the
Chicago tracks.

(who have been walked around the paddock) to go into their stalls, everybody knows "riders up" is coming pretty soon after that.

At first it was not comfortable for me to be in the spotlight like that, calling attention to myself when I was giving out orders. I was very uncomfortable for a while. But then that feeling left. I got over it. You've got a job to do. You're constantly watching the horses — you're so consumed with that that nothing else really matters out there. On Saturdays I used to get dressed up and wear heels in the paddock. I don't do that anymore. I know better. Flats all the time now, because I've been chased by horses, hit in the face by swishing tails — but never injured, yet. I'm pretty fleet afoot in there.

I grew up within two or three blocks of the tracks. The tracks, Sportsman's and Hawthorne, were just the big things. Now I live in Lemont (a town southwest of Chicago). I've been married for thirty years. My husband, Owen, trained. Now he works in the mutuels. My husband's family was involved in racing forever.

I was born June 12, 1949. My father was a mutuel clerk for, oh gosh, at least thirty years. My maiden name was Grzeskowiak. My grandfather and a couple of my uncles were policemen in Cicero. A couple of them worked in security at Hawthorne and Sportsman's.

You know what my first memory of the racetrack was? There used to be a little station wagon parked outside Sportsman's that a man and woman would sell hot dogs out of. They were the best hot

dogs! I will never have a hot dog as good in my whole entire life. They'd park their station wagon right on Laramie Avenue, and my grandmother would walk me over. You could smell those hot dogs cooking from a block and a half away. All the people from the neighborhood would come. Then, if they were running a race, you could stand right there and look through the spaces in the fence and see the horses. To grow up in a neighborhood like that, with the horses right here, well, it was great.

Cicero's just such a working-class town. Blocks of bungalows, just old-time tradition. You had such an ethnic mix — Polish and Italian and Irish. Cicero was pretty much noted for about every corner having a tavern. I remember my dad saying that you could walk down a block in the summer and pass the taverns and know what was going on in the races, because a lot of taverns booked the races then.

In this kind of industrial area, to have the tracks sitting right in the middle of all these homes and businesses, I think it was pretty unique. We'd see the horses going by through the fence. That was great for us kids. It got us interested. I remember that when I'm in the paddock in my job today, because any time you read an article about racing being on the decline it's because it's not attracting enough young people. I think we have to create our fan base from little kids, like what happened to me. I remember being in awe of horses.

I love it when a rider hands a pair of his goggles to a kid. You're helping to create a fan that way. That's what worries me about all the intertrack and simulcast wagering: I don't want this to just be a

TV thing. I love the people and the atmosphere at the track. It scares me the direction that a lot of this is going.

I used to ask my folks and my grandparents to take me to the track. I loved the horse aspect of it. We used to get big crowds back then. On Laramie Avenue the traffic used to be bumper to bumper over the bridge. As a kid, you just knew something great was going on over there at the track. And you wanted to be in on it.

My grandfather and my [future] father-in-law were very, very close friends. My grandfather would bring me to Ralph Salvino's barn on the weekends when I was just a little kid. I would ride on Ralph's stable pony. I came to realize years later that my [future] husband was around the stable then, too, of course. I never really knew Owen at that point in time.

I met my husband — really met him — when I was sixteen. Not at the track, either, but at a neighborhood carnival. I knew the family, but never *knew* the family — there were so doggone many of them! It was like you took a test when you met with him. We had a Christmas party just a week ago. We had to rent a hall. And that was just for the immediate family. I sat there; I was totally in awe. There were 116 of us, and a lot couldn't attend.

When Owen and I met, he was going to high school, but he'd be at the barn in the morning helping his dad. Then he'd go to school and come back to the barn to help out in the afternoon. He wanted to be a veterinarian. But he wound up going to Vietnam. When he came back, he ended up getting involved with the mutuels and training on his own.

We went to the high school prom. Owen was in charge of the barn in the morning. You know how you stay out all night after a prom? So there we were at the racetrack in the morning. We went to feed the horses with our prom clothes on — him in his tux, me in my gown. There we were in the barn feeding the horses. It had to be done, and that was it. They'd probably never been fed that early in the morning.

When Owen and I were dating, I helped out at his dad's barn, walking hots. I had a great relationship with Owen's dad. Everybody called him "Rocky," because he was the rock. He was seven days a week, 365 days a year, all his life. He'd be at the barn at four in the morning and eight at night. He still had a horse in training when he died. What was funny was that his wife and their four daughters, none of them had anything to do (directly) with racing. They could not understand how I could want to be back there working.

You don't realize until you get back there what is involved. I developed more respect for people. I've never seen a harder working bunch in my entire life. I don't know that there's too many jobs that you can even compare to this. There is nothing that stops you. You are going to get to that barn. I mean, you are dealing with living things. These aren't like wind-up toys.

When I got out of high school, I had office jobs. Dr. Duncan was building a veterinary clinic right across the street from the Hawthorne parking lot, and I wanted to work there. But before that opened, I was approached by Phil Langley. He was the racing secretary at the Sportsman's harness meeting, and they needed somebody in the office. Of course, with my love of the track it worked out great. I was twenty-one or twenty-two. I worked for them for seven years. Then a job came open at Sportsman's on the Thoroughbred side, typing the overnight (sheet of entries), working in the office. I've been with the Thoroughbreds ever since. I got to be (Sportsman's Park racing secretary) Tommy Scott's secretary.

It was Allison DeLuca (who was racing secretary at the time) that first made me a racing official. I was a patrol judge on the clubhouse turn, the first turn for the sprint races (prior to the reconfiguration of the Sportsman's racing strip). The horses broke right there. Watching that, watching the gate crew, I realized what a physical beating those guys take. It's incredible.

My job was to watch for infractions of any kind. Now, with television, we don't even have patrol judges out there in those stands anymore. TV cameras pick up every aspect of the race, every angle around the track.

There's a lot that goes on there in the first turn. There's a lot of yelling and screaming by the riders, and you're watching for horses coming over or bearing out, whatever, so that you can relay what you see to the stewards.

I was bad there. I really was. The first thing that you're told is that you never leave that stand during a race. But instinct sometimes takes over. There were spills in that first turn. One day Randy

Meier and Eddie King went down right in front of me. It was an awful spill. Randy was hurt very, very badly — bruised his heart, among other things. He hit so hard he was face down on the track.

Eddie King broke his leg, but he was able to roll under the rail. But Randy was there right on the racetrack. I really thought he was dying. I came down out of the stand and ran over to him. It was total instinct, just going out there. I tried to get his head out of the dirt so he could breathe. The horses were coming around. I was waving my arms, trying to get everybody over to the outside fence so they wouldn't run over Randy. It worked. Randy was hurt really bad, but he came back. He always comes back and does good. Thank God for that.

I was a patrol judge for two years. Then Allison asked me about being the paddock judge. I thought, "This is great. Now I'll have the closeness with the horses." I've been doing it ever since.

What I do first, before each race, is call the horses over (from the barns). When they get to the paddock, we check them to see if they're wearing blinkers if they're listed to wear them. Then, it's just basically getting all the horses saddled. We're on the clock. You want ten-minute post parades. If we have a horse lose a shoe in the paddock, we have to have the blacksmith work on him in there. You want all the horses to go out at the same time. They're all supposed to have their weight up for the same period of time. So, if I need to hold one horse in the paddock, to have a shoe put on for example, then I've got to hold them all in there. We've got to get everybody out of there in one piece. You're dealing with a lot of horses in a very compact area.

You make concessions. These horses have minds of their own. We've had some hellacious things happen. We've had horses rear up and go through the ceiling in the paddock.

The first time I had a two-year-old race, first-time starters, I was a nervous wreck. I thought, "Oh my God, this is going to be a nightmare." But it wasn't. What's really funny is that horses don't seem to show any bad traits until their second or third time in the paddock. The first time they come in there, they're wide-eyed. They're in awe. Looking around, they're like "what's going on here?" But the second or third time, they've started to get a sense of "wait a minute, I know what's coming." That's when you see the changes in them.

I had one horse who would not go out the regular entrance of the paddock at Sportsman's. Would not do it. He would absolutely plant all four feet and wouldn't budge. But I learned if I sent the rest of the field out first, we could get this horse to run out. That's the only way he would go, on the dead run. We used to have people running behind him in order to keep him moving out onto the track.

There was another horse who would not let himself be saddled. Every time you would go to throw the saddle on his back, this son of a gun would rear up in the air. One day I noticed that when the bugler would start playing the call to the post, this horse would all of a sudden start standing like he was in a trance. They could saddle him then.

So I told the trainer, "I might be crazy, but I've noticed that when the bugle plays you can do anything with this horse." What they ended up doing is they put the bugle call on a cassette tape, and they would bring that into the paddock every time this horse ran. They would turn on the tape, he'd go into his trance, and they'd saddle him. They never had a problem with him after that. It was beautiful.

With problem horses, the trainers are very receptive to getting suggestions. They don't want problems, either. It's helping them out not having to fight their horse, maybe getting somebody hurt in the process.

I have been fortunate to learn the different aspects of racing. When you know what goes on on a daily basis on the backside, you've got in the back of your mind that you don't know what this or that poor guy might have gone through during the night with one of his horses. So you keep that in mind in the way you treat them.

On the whole, the horsemen are wonderful. They want to do the right things. There are days when I have a long list of people who want to school their horses (in the paddock). You always try to accommodate them. You want them to come in there with the horses and work with them. It's for everybody's benefit, really.

I had a horse that came in to school one day between races. She was the only horse in the paddock. I was in my (nearby) office and all of a sudden it sounded like the walls were caving in. She'd thrown a fit, reared over backwards, and hit her head on a pole. She died right there, in the paddock, while a race was going on.

Now, I've got other horses coming into the paddock for the next race. And I've got this dead horse laying there. There was blood everywhere — on the walls, on the vets; it was the most horrendous thing I'd ever seen.

How do you get a dead horse out of the paddock? At Sportsman's, the crowd in the paddock is right there, close up. But the hoist on the (horse) ambulance wasn't working. I've got to keep the other horses from coming in, so I ran to the back of the paddock and kept them there and that's where they saddled. I finally get about five guys who drag this horse out of the paddock. A three- or four-year-old filly. She just acted silly, and it was an awful thing. You never get used to that part of it. Or the breakdowns, and the riders getting hurt.

I work six days a week. We're dark (no racing) Mondays and Tuesdays, but we work on Mondays taking entries. It's every weekend, every holiday. It was hard for me to adjust to holidays, especially now with my grandson. Easter is hard for me, not being there for Easter morning with my family.

My grandson loves horses. When he comes to the track, he gets a ride from Ginger the pony girl, just like his mother used to. He loves *The Black Stallion* movie. He's watched it a lot. Anthony knows it by heart. He acts it out; he's the Black Stallion, he's in the race, he gets hurt; it's hilarious. He's just three years old. When he plays like this, I have to say, "They're in the gate…and they're off," then he's off running around the house. But if I don't say "the flag is up," he won't run. We don't even use a flag man at the track anymore, but they did in the movie, and Anthony wants the flag man.

I think my husband thinks my job is pretty neat. I mean, after all, from the time we were kids together we were around horses.

When I started as paddock judge, my husband was still training. I was probably harder on him and his family than anybody else. I made absolutely sure my husband and the rest of them that I dealt with were cut no slack. They had better do everything perfect or they'd hear about it from me (laughs). I caught myself maybe being too tough on them. Owen never said anything, but I caught myself.

The other day, we were getting ready to go out for dinner. When Owen got home from work, I asked him what he had to do to get ready, and he said he wanted to take a bath before we went. So I said to him, "It's late. Get in there and do it." And he said back to me, "You're not in the paddock, you know."

We had to laugh. Sometimes I might bring my work home with me and not know it.

DONNA PORTER

$\mathcal{T}$raveling Team

Donna Porter was once the youngest corporate vice president of the giant Bank of America Corporation. Today, she is as far removed from that world as she is from her native state of California, where her banking career started and ended. She and her husband, Max, work together as racing officials at Midwestern tracks, traveling to as many as four each year. Donna says she "wouldn't have it any other way. There are so many exciting things in racing. Every day is a new day!"

Born in 1948, Porter was raised in a rural area near Los Angeles. Her fondness for horses developed at an early age, and she grew into an avid participant in horse shows. "I learned to ride before I could walk," she said.

After earning a degree in English literature from Cal State-Northridge, Porter entered banking. She married Arkansas native Max Porter in 1971. Max owned and ran a California boarding and breeding farm with the motto: "Dedicated to Fast Horses and Those

Donna Porter gave up a
banking career to work
on the racetrack.

Who Love Them." In 1988 Max sold the farm, and with Donna as his partner, he began training at tracks in the Southwest and Midwest.

Six years later, when their major patron retired, the Porters became officials. Donna is a placing judge and entry clerk at Hawthorne Race Course, Ellis Park, Oaklawn Park, and Kentucky Downs. Max, too, works in the racing secretary's office and usually serves as a placing and/or patrol judge at their many yearly stops.

In their time away from the track, the Porters, who have a home in Evansville, Indiana, frequently travel. They have taken a cross-country trip on Max's motorcycle, traversed the continent by car, and sailed the waters of the Pacific off the coast of California in their own boat. "Our favorite word," Donna said, "is 'go.' "

The Porters are also avid readers and dedicated book collectors: they own more than 2,500 volumes. Their collection includes numerous rare first editions of works by authors such as J.D. Salinger (Catcher in the Rye), *Charles Dickens, Robert Browning, and Margaret Mitchell* (Gone With the Wind). *In their avocation as bibliophiles and vocation as racing officials, Donna said, "Max and I work as a team in a life we both really enjoy."*

When I graduated from college in 1969, my mom sent me and two of my girlfriends to Hawaii as a graduation present. I decided to stay there for the summer. I got a job selling tickets to the Don Ho show. That's where I met Max — I sold him a ticket to the show. I'll never forget it: He had this long hair and dark glasses, and it was nighttime, and he was wearing this cap that said "Max Porter Training," or "Max Porter Thoroughbreds," and I thought, "What an interesting guy." He invited me for drinks after the show. We had a nice time, but then his Hawaiian vacation was over, and he went back to California.

I went back [to California] in the fall. One day I was driving near my home and spotted this gorgeous two-door Jaguar convertible that had a bale of hay sticking out of its trunk. That caught my eye. Then I saw it was Max driving — he was on his way to his farm. I honked my horn, stopped, and we talked. We started to date not long after that — it turned out we lived only four miles from each other — and we were married in 1971. It was fate. We've had a great life together ever since.

I got started in the banking business after graduation from college. When I graduated, I thought I would go into teaching. But it was the late 1960s, early '70s; people weren't having babies, and there just weren't any teaching jobs available for me.

So I started interviewing for jobs, and I got hired by United Bank of California. They had a job opening for a brand new thing involving computers and putting companies' accounts payable reports and so on into a computer system. This was all a new area for the bank. The computers then were as big as houses.

We'd go out and gather information. A whole team of us would hit a big company, and then we'd come back with all our information written down. We'd punch it onto little cards, and then out would come these reports. That's what I did when I started with the bank, and I liked it so much. It was all new and fabulous, and we got to travel. Then, after I had been with UCB for about five years, Bank of America offered me a job to run this whole program for them.

I was head of a department called business services. We dealt with the bank's top customers. One of the accounts I had was Nissan, a huge company. I would take a whole team out there. At one time, I had fifty people working for me. My team was among the first to develop the field of human resources, where you tracked the company's employees and information on them. Before, with an employee, a company would know his starting date and his birth date and if he was married; that was about it. With human resources, other things were coming into play because of the things that were happening with benefits, the IRAs, 401(k) plans, all of that. So putting all this onto a computer and writing all this technology and language...well, you were making it up as you went. It was a fun thing. That was probably one of the most challenging things I ever did in my life.

In 1988, after I'd worked for the banks for more than ten years, Max and I decided we wanted to see more of the country. We decided to hit the road. He said, "Let's leave California and see what's out there."

So he put together a public stable and for several years we raced all over — Turf Paradise, Albuquerque, Ak-Sar-Ben, Ohio,

Kentucky, The Woodlands. We had a horse that won a stakes at The Woodlands. Then we moved to Kentucky and Max went private, training for Roselawn Farm until the owner, Pam McArdle, decided to retire.

My husband was training, and I was helping him with the barn thing. We never had more than twenty head because we liked to do all the work. We were really hands on. Max has always had his own horse trailer, and if it took us five trips to move the stable from one track to the next, we made five trips, because he would never let anybody van them.

My connection with horses was forever. When I was four or five years old, my grandfather got me a little donkey called Cactus. That was my first rideable animal. We always had horses. We lived in Woodland Hills, near the Warner [Brothers] ranch northwest of Los Angeles. It was huge — miles and miles of walnut groves, cornfields; you could ride over it forever.

My dad built me a little barn at the back of our property. We had about an acre. After I had the donkey, my grandfather was determined to get me a horse. My grandpa was the best. He loved horses, the West, and he had this friend, Harry Hill, who lived near us. Harry was truly an old-time cowboy. All the Western movie stars used to hang out at Harry Hill's. My grandpa told Harry, "We've got to get this girl a horse."

One day Harry brought over this big old white horse named Stormy. Harry rode it over, then jumped off the horse's butt onto the ground. Then Harry bent down and duck walked between the horse's legs to show my grandpa how safe this horse would be for me. That's how I got Stormy.

When I was seven or eight, one of my girlfriends said to me, "We've got to start going to some of these horse shows. We should be getting ready to get in them."

So we'd come home after school and work with our horses. My dad had built a little ring for me to ride in. We're trying to jump over things, and open gates — trail horses were real big then.

I rode to my first horse show, a pretty long way, wearing jeans and a hat — all stuff that I had made myself. I had a saddle by now; I even made that. It was just like some strips of leather. I'll never forget that day. There were sixty-three people in my event in this horse show. It was like a trail event. You had to go through gates and over a pond and back your horse up and drop the reins and walk away from the horse while it stood there.

All of the other people in the event were dressed in stuff to die for. They've got chaps and so on — they looked like people who should be in horse shows. Here's me in my little outfit that I made. But I got third place! After that, my dad said, "We've got to get this kid some riding gear." And he did. For years, my whole life was horse shows. That's what I did all the time.

I got into show jumping after the Western part. In Western (competition), you were judged. If you got a judge that didn't like the horse or didn't like the way you looked — well, it was real subjective. So I switched over to jumping. We'd go to a place every Saturday night in Burbank. You'd put money in a pot. The rider who had the best time and knocked down the fewest jumps got the money. It was clear-cut.

It's funny because, although we didn't know it at the time, Max was probably at some of the same shows I was at during some of that time. He lived in that area, and he used to go to them. So we probably saw each other years before we knew each other.

Max is the most amazing person. When he was training, if there was a horse that wasn't right, Max would sit there and watch that animal. He'd pull up a little chair and watch, and he would always figure out what was going on — why it wasn't eating, if it needed something. I can honestly say that my husband never knowingly ran a horse that was sore. He would just tell the owner he couldn't do it and "if you're not happy with that, take the horse to somebody else." I always felt so good about that because these animals look to you for everything. Gosh, you've got to love them.

We had a horse named Throw a Natural, who Max bought when we were at The Woodlands. We called him Nate. He was the most gorgeous animal you have ever seen. When you look at the old English oil paintings, you know that beautiful, majestic look they have? That is how this horse looked. He was a bay, with just a little bit of white on his back feet.

The young guy Max bought him from couldn't win a race with

him. He'd claimed him in Phoenix, but it seemed Nate couldn't find his way up the racetrack. He was seven or eight years old. But Max said, "We'll buy him because he's so pretty."

And he was such a character. This is such poor horsemanship that I shouldn't even say it, but Nate did not like a lead rope, so we didn't use one. He would just follow behind us anywhere we were walking.

Nate had some other quirks, too. He had to be in the first stall of our shed row. I know this sounds stupid, but if you put him in a stall down the row, he went berserk. He had to be in the stall right next to our little office.

You had to put his food and water up at the front of the stall because he never went to the back of the stall. And he hated webbing on the stall. If you put a webbing up, he would paw and bite it. If you shut the bottom half of the door, he would kick it. All he wanted was one little strip of rubber to be placed across the door opening. That was fine with him. He would never crawl under it or go out.

People would tell me, "Donna, you are going to get into trouble not putting a webbing on his stall," and I knew it. I am a good horseman. But I couldn't do it. This animal...I never had anything like him in my life.

So we brought him back to Phoenix. Nate was training good, and we put him in and he runs second. Max said, "I know what's wrong with him — he hits himself." His front feet were hitting his back feet when he ran. So we bring in this horseshoer who we always used, and he put these special shoes on Nate. He made them higher on the inside and lower on the outside. So, we put him back in and Nate wins easy.

That was what Max was good at — figuring them out. The guy we bought the horse from came over after the race and says, "How did you do that?" Max said, "We just fixed his feet." That race was Throw a Natural's one-hundredth career start. The newspaper in Phoenix did a story on him. Everybody loved him. When we retired him, we sent him to California to a family we knew and he became a real good hunter-jumper. That's another thing about my husband, Max always tried to make sure that when our horses were done racing they went to good places.

I enjoyed the years Max was training. We made a lot of friends. If people were in trouble and needed something, you really helped them. If someone was sick, you took care of them. And when you wished them luck, you meant it. Because, you know, it was a family on the backstretch. I am not so sure it's still that way. I think it's become more cutthroat today. Still, compared to other businesses, I'd say the camaraderie that exists among horse people is pretty exceptional.

I first worked in the racing office at Pomona in California, the Fairplex meet (after quitting the bank and getting married). But then Max started training, and we hit the road. I was helping him, so it wasn't until about 1994 that I got back into it. We were at Ellis Park. They were shorthanded in the secretary's office there one day, and they sent someone to the backside asking if I could work in the racing office. Once I got in there, I just stayed with it.

When Max retired from training, the same thing happened to him, and this was at Ellis Park, too, the next year. They needed somebody with computer skills to work on the track program. The person that was doing it had just walked in one day and said, "I quit." Max was in the track kitchen when we called him and said, "Could you come up here?" He did, and he picked it up right away. He'd already had computer courses. That's how the two of us got into this work permanently.

We both help take entries in the mornings at all the tracks we work. Max is a patrol judge at Oaklawn and a placing judge at the other tracks. I'm a placing judge at all of them. I also put together the track programs at Hawthorne and Ellis, and I'm the claims clerk at Ellis. I have a lot of variety; I do a little bit of everything. In the mornings I love to answer that phone and say, "Good morning, Racing Office."

When I first met my husband, women were really not allowed on the backside. I can remember him having to sign me in every morning at the stable gate. And you couldn't be back there after dark. I don't remember any women in the racing secretaries' offices at all in those days. So a lot has changed over the years. Women love horses. Any woman that has grown up around horses, it is a natural thing to carry that interest on to the racetrack. But we don't really do enough to bring women into the racing world. I think women are very depend- able — they have great follow-through habits, organizational skills —

and that is what started to come across to the men who ran racing.

At Hawthorne I run the computer that records where the horses finished in their races. This used to be done with photographs, but now it's computers. The computer captures every horse as it hits the wire, places the horses from first to last, the distances between them, and gives the individual times that they cross the wire. Then that information goes to make up the official chart of each race, and after that it goes into each horse's past performance line. It's a good system and very quick. It's good for the betting public, because it lets you put the finish photo up right away. You can enlarge that photo just by clicking the "plus" button on the computer.

We had a photo finish at Hawthorne a couple of years ago (1999) that I'll never forget. It was one of the big races, the (grade III, $200,000) National Jockey Club Handicap. Baytown and Precocity hit the wire together. Both trainers — Niall O'Callaghan trained Baytown, and Bobby Barnett trained Precocity — congratulated each other because neither knew who had won.

It took us (she and the two other placing judges) eight minutes to determine that Baytown had won. That's the longest photo I can remember. You have to be so careful — there's so much at stake. After we put up the numbers, both trainers wanted to come upstairs to our office and see the photo. We welcome that. Bobby Barnett looked at the photo and said, "Good call. There's a whisker between those two." That's what we love to hear. It's so important that we make the right decision.

That eight-minute photo will probably never happen again. This technology enables us to decide the outcome very fast in most cases. And that's good. People want to know the result and then move on and start handicapping the next race. Speeding things up is important. In horse racing, you've got to start bringing in younger people. Young people want things fast. They don't want to wait.

I love all aspects of my job — the afternoons at the computer, the mornings with people. Max and I are usually the first ones arriving in the racing office every morning. It's probably a carry-over from Max's training days. I like working with people, and that's what you get in the racing office — trainers, jockey agents, owners, everybody.

You want to be pleasant to people and make sure they are getting what they need — especially owners. Horse owners are so important to this game. If we don't have owners, none of us have jobs. You've got to treat them nicely. Especially the new owners that come into the office; they don't know the routine yet. You should be saying to them, "Hi, can I help you?" Not looking at them like you're thinking, "What, you want a condition book? You frigging fool."

These people are paying the bills! And this is an expensive business!

We had some new owners come in the other day. Brand new people; brought all their kids out. They sat out there looking bewildered, no one helping them, so I walked out from behind the counter and said, "You guys need any help with anything?" They said they were new, they'd gotten their [racing] colors that day, and they wanted to get licensed. So I showed them what to do.

Max and I work about ten months every year, but it's usually six days a week, so we need our two months off. People say to us, "How can you stand so much traveling (from track to track)? Why do you do it?" I tell them that every track is different. We meet people everywhere that you could write books about.

I feel lucky that I can do something that I can't wait to start doing every day. I look at people who think, "Oh, I've got to go to work today," and I know how lucky I am. Because I can't wait to get there!

Max and I are so fortunate to have each other. Every day I say to him, "I am so lucky to have you." I mean, it brings tears to my heart. He is a great person and so much fun. If we see somebody along the road, he'll stop to help. If we see a dog that is stranded on the highway, he'll go back and pick it up. He is just like that. I have never in my life met anybody like him.

To me, life's all about having fun and letting people know that you enjoyed meeting them, that you have enjoyed being with them. Because let me tell you, in the racing business you are going to see them down the road, at the next track. Oh, maybe not this year, but you will see them some place and they will remember you. That's my whole thing in life — that I hope that I am remembered for treating somebody good.

CHAPTER 13

SHERYL   STEFANOWICZ

$\mathcal{N}$ine Stories a Day

S*heryl Stefanowicz holds one of Thoroughbred racing's most responsible jobs. Yet most bettors are unaware of what she does as a chart caller, which is to produce a detailed description of each race run at the track where she works. These reports include facts and commentaries that make up the official chart of each race. The chart, in turn, leads to past performance lines that provide the wagering public with information about the horses.*

When she tries to explain what she does, Stefanowicz said people "usually have no clue. They probably think it's a computer going boop, boop, boop, churning out the charts."

The Daily Racing Form *began to employ a few women to call the charts in the 1980s. But women remained a relative rarity until the 1990 advent of Equibase, now the official keeper of Thoroughbred racing statistics in North America. Equibase executive Chuck Scaravilli Jr. in 2000 listed some two-dozen women who now call*

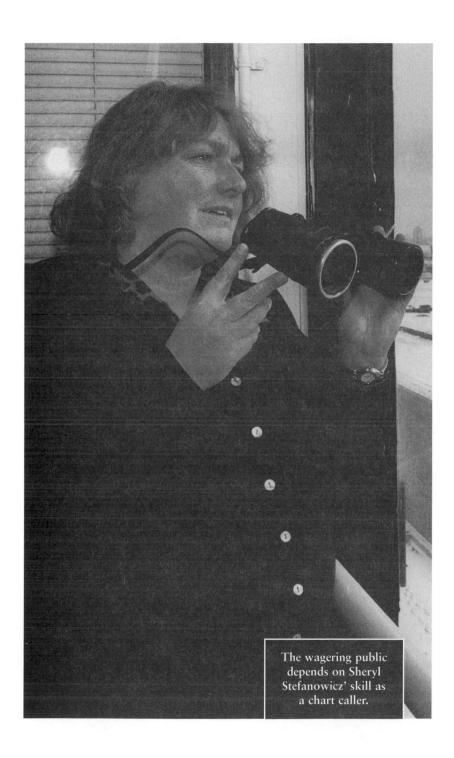

The wagering public depends on Sheryl Stefanowicz' skill as a chart caller.

charts at U.S. tracks. Stefanowicz was a member of one of Equibase's first training classes.

Born in Chicago in 1957, she is the daughter of the late Daily Racing Form clocker Jack Rogers. He introduced her to racing when she was a child, then helped her get a job at the racetrack when she was a teenager. In the ensuing years, and following her marriage to Ed Stefanowicz, a Chicago ironworker, Stefanowicz has continued to work in racing.

M y first job at the racetrack was as a tab writer for the clockers. It was the summer before I started at Northern (Illinois University). A tab writer is the first job you take if you want to be a clocker. It's the person who writes down the information — the horse's name, how far, and how fast he worked — called out by the clockers. What you're doing is compiling all the names and the times and typing them up. You're just kind of like a secretary to the clockers. When I did that, I was able to be done with work by noon, and I made some money.

It was through an uncle of mine that my dad got taken on as a clocker. He would get up early every morning — you've got to be out here by five every morning — and do his clocking, then three afternoons a week he'd go for dialysis. That was before he got the transplant. He started his clocking here at Arlington (Park, in the Chicago suburb of Arlington Heights).

My dad was interested in racing before that — he had been to the track a lot of times and, yes, he liked to bet. Not too much, 'cause we didn't have very much, but he used his little extra money. He knew some gamblers that went to the track a lot. That's how he first got interested. He and I would go to the track together. We both liked it a lot.

When I started working, I rode with my dad in his car to the track every morning; then he would bring me home after the job was done. Most of the time, I'd sleep on the ride there and the ride back. At the beginning, my dad would tell me every day to keep my mouth shut. He'd say, "Just be quiet. Just do your work." At first I felt out of place, because you think you know everything when you're that age, twenty or so. And you think others don't know anything. You know what I'm saying? I would see them (fellow workers) doing stuff, and I'm thinking, "I could do that." And then as you get older, you know that you know nothing (laughs).

They'd start clocking every morning as soon as it got light out. Here at Arlington, we would always sit outside. I would watch and try to learn what they were doing. The clockers would call out the names of the horses working, and I would write them down on these big pieces of paper they used then. They'd be so good at identifying horses, which is really an art.

They'd call out, "I got this horse at the five-eighths pole; I got this horse breaking off on the turn." They'd identify them from their saddle towels, or if they had jocks and were going to work (work out), or from memory.

You'd identify horses by whether they were colts or geldings or fillies, by their color, by their exercise riders, or by their equipment. You'd say, "Okay, here comes five bays all with the same trainer. Who wears blinkers?" You'd look in the book. Does the horse have a full hood? Some other piece of equipment? That's how you would narrow it down. This is in a good world, when it's not that busy. There are also people at the gaps (entrances from the barn area to the oval) leading into the track who are getting horses' names for you.

But it can be pretty hectic. After the first break of the morning (during which the racing strip is cleared of horses and harrowed), there would be a lot of horses breaking from the gate. There'd be twenty or thirty horses working at the same time at different points around the track. The clockers have to be on top of them. They have to see every horse that's working. Sometimes six would pop out of the gate. But the old clockers, they were just calm about it.

There'd be trainers sometimes that would work their horses in the dark. But usually there'd be a clocker way up there in the stands who saw them. Sometimes a trainer would use saddle towels that weren't really his, or he'd tell you a name for a horse that wasn't really its name. But you couldn't fool those clockers.

Once I started working here in the mornings, I started to really appreciate it more. It's just such a different experience than in the afternoon. In the mornings, early, a lot of time there's fog or mist, and there's so many horses on the track, not just eight or nine like for a race. You see hundreds of horses and exercise riders and pony people; everybody just doing their thing, and it kind of draws you in. It's hard to break the habit of it.

I was one of the first woman clockers; I was a girl, really. I didn't think of it in terms of, "well, I'm a woman doing this." People never tried to make me feel uncomfortable, so I didn't feel uncomfortable, and it never became an issue. You just had better do your job and get on with it instead of letting any kind of male/female thing get in the way. So that's what I did.

When I first started, besides my dad, other clockers were a couple of old black men, Hunchy (William Barber) and Pete (Peterson). They must have been eighty and ninety years old; at least it seemed like it to me. Hunchy's nickname? I guess he used to have kind of a tout sheet that he'd sell in the afternoons; maybe it had to do with hunch bets. They would let clockers have sheets like that then. That's where his name came from. There's a lot of colorful names on the racetrack, all over the place.

Pete, the older one, he had been one of the best clockers anywhere — that's what my dad said. He clocked for years and years. When he got older, his eyesight went bad. So, he couldn't clock anymore, but he kept on working. He would type up the work tab (summary) that would be sent into the *Racing Form* to be published. Pete wouldn't trust anybody else to type it up. He couldn't see well enough to copy down what I'd written on the work tab, so I would sit next to him and spell out every single name for him to type on one of those old-fashioned typewriters. It took a long time every day, but that was the way Pete wanted to do it. So we did. I didn't mind it. You work with people every day, under pressure, in a tiny space, you get to know them. Hunchy and Pete were very good to me — they were like my grandpas.

When Hunchy died, I think I was twenty. My dad and I drove to his wake, way down on the south side of Chicago. We were the only white people there. Hunchy's wife gave all his stopwatches to my father. That was quite a thing.

(Editors' note: Following college, Sheryl tried some office jobs that she didn't particularly like and soon returned to the track as a clocker in the mornings, also serving as official timer in the afternoons and working in the publicity department at the Chicago tracks. Late in the autumn of 1990 a new career opportunity presented itself.)

I had learned to use computers — to send entries and results and so on. The older guys in the publicity departments were starting to retire; they'd rather retire than learn the computers. So I learned them.

When Equibase started, I was working in publicity at Hawthorne. Equibase was a new company that was going to start charting races and making past performances. They were in competition with the *Form*. The racetracks helped finance Equibase. The tracks wanted to own their own information and statistics so they wouldn't have to rely on the *Form* for all of that anymore.

That was in the fall of 1990. Equibase wanted to have a chart caller ready to go the next February when Sportsman's Park opened their meeting. John Brokopp at Hawthorne and Mike Paradise at Sportsman's, the publicity directors, they were looking for someone to do the job. They thought I could do it. Mr. Bidwill (Charles "Stormy" Bidwill, chairman of Sportsman's Park) thought I could do it. They called me in one day and said, "Do you want to go to Cincinnati and learn how to do this job? It's going to pay a bunch of money." (laughs)

This was a tremendous opportunity for me. They had confidence in me, Stormy and C-3 (Charles W. Bidwill, the Sportsman's Park president and Stormy's son). They said, "Here's a check. Go do it."

That was a very scary experience for me. I had a little bit of experience taking the chart calls, but it was very casual, just kind of filling in, seeing if I could do it. I had never called a race, where you have to report the position of every horse and what they're doing and what's happening to them. I had watched John Brown (the veteran chart caller in Chicago) work for years, and he was so professional; he was so good at the job. I had never thought of the possibility that I might try to do the same job. But there I was, and I had the support of the Bidwills, and I thought, "Well, I'm going to try. And if I'm no good at it, then I'm no good at it." But I was scared.

So I went to Cincinnati where Equibase was training people to go to work calling charts. Chuck Scaravilli Jr. was the big Kahuna; he ran the training program, and he was the nicest guy. He said, "Don't worry, we're going to do this." And Marshall Cassidy (long-time announcer at Aqueduct, Belmont Park, and Saratoga) was there with Chuck training us. They brought in people from about fifteen tracks around the country to try out for the jobs. Some of them were track announcers; some people had worked for the *Racing Form* calling races. I didn't have that background, the calling of the races. We would sit in class every day. There was one other girl in the class.

In the classroom during the days, they'd show us tapes of races and tell us what we should be looking for. Then we'd go to Turfway Park — at night! This was in December. We'd have our tape recorders, and we'd be standing out on the roof at Turfway Park. It was cold and it was dark! I was having trouble with my glasses (binoculars). And we'd watch races, live ones, but we'd look for the same things we did in the classroom. Chuck would say, "What happened there at the start?" Or, "What happened when they went into the second turn?" And we'd practice calling the races into our tape recorders. Then the next day Chuck and Marshall would go over the tapes with us, telling us what we did right and wrong. It was very intense training for one whole week, every day and night. Not everybody passed the course. Some people just couldn't do it.

When I got back to Chicago from Cincinnati, I went to meet with Mr. Bidwill (C-3). He said, "Well, do you think you can do it?' " And I said, "Well, I think so. I'm sure going to try."

For a while I went back to working in the publicity department at Hawthorne. There were still a couple of weeks of their meeting left — they ran to the end of the year.

So during the races I would sit in the announcer's booth with Phil Georgeff (longtime Chicago track announcer). I would just watch and listen. I was so scared, believe me. I was terrified that I wouldn't be able to do the job of calling races right. And I would practice like a little kid, quiet, alongside Phil. And I kept doing that.

After the New Year, all the new Equibase callers got time to get their feet wet. We'd call races and send the charts into headquarters, but they weren't being published yet. This was when they were just giving us time to get ready. I would work near Mr. Brown, and the first practice race I called into my tape recorder was a disaster. I said, "I don't know anything about these horses, and I don't know one thing to say." I was like, "Oh, I'm going to cry."

But the guys were very supportive. Mr. Brown always said to me, "You worry to death. You worry to death." They — John Brown, Bill Cassidy (another *Daily Racing Form* trackman) — were nice enough to give me encouragement. And they'd give me suggestions, "Why don't you put this in? Why don't you try this?" until I got the confidence to do the job.

In that time, when I was practicing and my charts weren't yet being printed by Equibase in the track programs, I'd call the same race Mr. Brown did. I learned a lot watching him, because he was really good at what he did. After a while I realized I was getting it. And when you do it over and over and over again, you get good at it.

I think the chart caller's job is to tell nine stories a day. A story for every race. Each race is a story unto itself, and that's what we're trying to do. We're trying to be exact with the facts, but trying to tell a story.

You have to concentrate when the race is being run. Then you can go back and watch the taped replay of the race — you're looking for something you might have missed or maybe taking a closer look at something you thought you saw. So you zero in on that. What you are trying to do is to help the public in terms of what you can tell them, positive or negative, about that race. We dissect the race; we're watching each horse and what it does, and watching the group as a whole.

Does the betting public have any concept of what I do? I don't think so. They probably think it's a computer going boop, boop, boop, churning out the charts. When I started out, I don't think I thought much about having a responsibility to the bettors — you know, to give them the best information I could. And I didn't think that much about it when I was going through that practice time before my charts were being printed. But when that happened, from the first day, when I realized that people were paying good money to read my charts and the past-performance lines they went into, well, I took it very seriously. I still do, believe me. What I'm doing is telling what the horses did last time, so that hopefully the bettors can get an idea of what they might do next time. We try to give them the best information possible.

If somebody I meet finds out I work at the track, they always think I'm a mutuel clerk. If I try to explain what I do, usually they have no clue. They have no concept of all the cogs in the wheel at the racetrack. Sometimes, after I've said I'm a chart caller, and they ask me again what I do, I'll take their program or their *Racing Form* and show them the information on each horse, and I'll say, "That's what I do. All this stuff here and all this stuff there, that's what I do."

And then it's always, "Do you have any tips?" And here's what I always say: "No, I can't bet." It's not that there's a rule against it. I used to bet, working around all the tracks I worked at. But I found out that when I started calling charts, betting just distracted me. It really distracted me. Your horse is at the back, and you're watching him, and he's not going anywhere; or he's starting to move, and you find you're missing the big picture of the race.

In a six-furlong race, you're giving the start call — where every horse was after the gate opened — and you have a quarter-mile call, half-mile call, stretch call, and the finish. If you see trouble, you say "circle this horse, or check this horse, or this horse had a bad trip." If you've got twelve horses going six furlongs, everything happens so quick. You're doing all this in this little itty-bitty bit of time.

We see some racing accidents, and you always feel bad. When a horse breaks down, you see the human attachment; there's a tremendous attachment between the horses and the grooms and the exercise riders and the owners and trainers. You hate to see horses getting hurt.

And, yes, there's pressure in the job. No matter how long you do it. After a big day, like an Arlington Million day, or the day Cigar was here, you have to kind of decompress. You don't really get nervous anymore, because you're confident. But on days like that, there's so much commotion going on. You have to let go of it. It's not brain surgery that you're doing, but you have to learn to let it go.

We (she and her husband) have a boat and a condo at Fox Lake (Illinois). I have to work weekends, which is the worst thing about the job, so I miss a lot of stuff. But I love going to the lake. I get there and go outside right away, and I sit and read, or veg, or I go in my Jacuzzi and have a glass of wine. Probably have a glass of wine first (laughs).

The one bad thing about the job is that you can't take a sick day. That's true with about every job on the racetrack. I mean I've come in to work with broken limbs and broken joints. When my brother got married, I had to ask the company to fly somebody in to cover for me. This job is so specialized, there's nobody who can just step in and take over and do it for you. So you never take a day off that you don't schedule way, way in advance. You just don't.

But I love the job. Working on weekends, that's the worst thing, but other than that it's a tremendous job, and the company's been very good to me. It's a good company to work for. We get a pension. We get a 401(k). We get health insurance. Most people working at the racetrack don't get all those things, believe me.

I think the best thing (about the job) is that I get to sit outside and look at the racetrack all day. And the people that you work with, it's like a community of people who like racing. I think people — I mean people outside racing — would be amazed at how this is a little world, a community.

When I was a kid, I never read books about horses. But now I understand their beauty and their power and what they go through in order to become a racehorse. It's an amazing process. And it's an amazing thing to be a good racehorse, let alone any racehorse! There's just so much to it.

Z O E   C A D M A N

*B*old and Determined

The first female jockey to be inducted into the National Museum of Racing's Hall of Fame was Julie Krone. By far the most successful of the few hundred women who have had riding careers in this country, Krone made history with her induction at Saratoga Springs, New York in the summer of 2000.

Zoe Cadman hails from a country in which women not only don't win awards but rarely are even permitted to compete at the professional level. And it was that lack of opportunity in England that brought her to the United States, where she launched her professional career with a winning ride aboard Prize and Joy at Arlington Park on June 10, 2000.

Born in South Africa, Cadman moved as a child with her parents to England. A self-described "unenthusiastic student," she nevertheless graduated from high school at age fifteen. When she was seventeen, she left home for good to seek work at Newmarket, England's

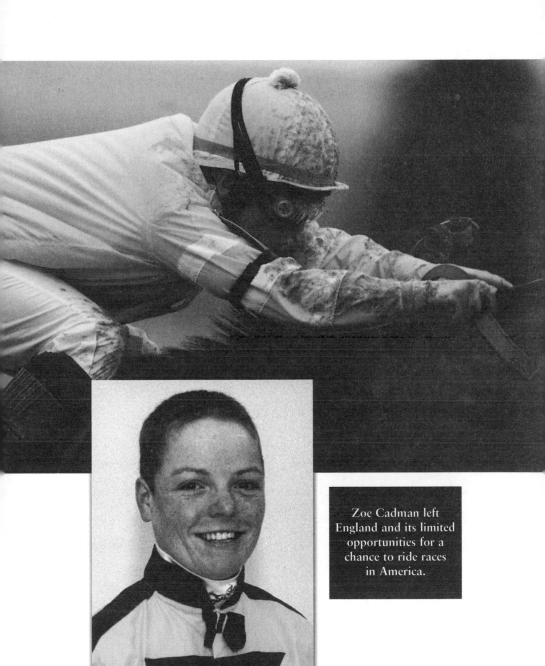

Zoe Cadman left England and its limited opportunities for a chance to ride races in America.

famous training center. She arrived in the United States in 1994 and joined trainer Michael Dickinson's staff as an exercise rider. Cadman served subsequent stints with trainers Chris Speckert and Michael Stidham before becoming a jockey.

After her victorious debut, Cadman did well at Arlington Park before being injured in a mishap behind the starting gate. Sidelined for six weeks, she returned with a flourish, and on September 16, 2000, became the first woman rider in Arlington history to win three races on one program. (Because of the injury, her apprenticeship was extended until August 2001.) That led to her winning the track's Rising Star award. Cadman went on to Hawthorne Race Course where she placed third in the standings with forty-six victories as her mounts earned $824,843.

Cadman's annual circuit now leads from the Chicago tracks to the New Orleans Fair Grounds and back. At the 2001 Sportsman's Park meeting that concluded April 30, Cadman won twenty-three races — good for sixth place in the standings — and more than a half-million dollars in purses. For most of the year, Cadman makes her home in Palatine, Illinois.

I was born in 1974 Johannesburg, South Africa. My parents are English, and they moved back to England when I was six. Mom had gotten homesick, but as soon as she got back to England, she was missing the maids and the house and the swimming pool and that kind of stuff they had in South Africa. But they couldn't go back. My dad does computers; that's why they were there in the first place.

I have a twin brother — Ro. He's in England. He's married, has two kids. He has no interest in horses. Also, he's about five-foot-eleven, while I'm five feet.

We always had horses around when I was growing up. I had ponies as a kid, did all the Pony Club stuff. I basically just grew up doing show jumping and cross-country and dressage — which I hated. I found dressage too boring. I wanted to go fast. But dressage was one of the things we had to do.

I had a pony called Thunder, who was a little shit. I had some others, too. The first one I bought cost 420 pounds, and he was my last pony. He was like a mini-Thoroughbred. He was eighteen years old and only had three good legs, but he could run fast. His license said he was a pony, but he was actually 15.1 hands. His name was Oliver. I saved up and paid about half what he cost to buy.

I had a great time growing up in England. My parents gave me a free rein to do whatever I wanted to, and I had fun.

But I hated school. I left school when I was fifteen. I always just wanted to work with horses. I didn't see how there was any reason for me to know how to do X minus Z plus Y; that was of no use to me whatsoever. Although I wished I'd learned long division, because I can't divide anything (laughs).

When I finished high school, I went to be a working pupil for a woman named Clarissa Strawn who had a stable in Devon.

Basically, you worked your ass off and you didn't get paid. It was actually the best thing I could have done. I moved out from home. There were five of us girls living in a cottage on the [Strawn] farm. And we just went nuts; we had a blast. I mean, we'd start working at five in the morning and get done at seven at night. We had to buy our own food. But I had a great time. We used to get on a lot of steeplechase horses and flat horses to break — that's when I first got interested in flat (racing) horses. We used to have lessons every day, and Clarissa used to yell at us. I stayed there a year, a year and a half, and I learned a lot.

When I was sixteen or so, I decided that if I were going to ride flat races, I had better get to Newmarket. So, I wrote letters to every trainer based at Newmarket. I got only one answer, from a guy named Sir Mark Prescott. He was like, "I'd be delighted for you to come and work for me." I went down and met him. It was my first job interview, and I was chatting away with him. I basically couldn't shut up. I was like yap, yap, yap. That was the most I ever spoke to Sir Mark. Because after that, the day of my interview when he hired me, he basically never spoke to me again (laughs).

I remember walking into his yard the first morning after the job interview. It was in April, and I said, "Hey, Mark, how are you doing?" And he pulls me aside and says, "You have to call me 'sir.'" And then I found out that his yard was one of the strictest in Newmarket. You had to wear jodhpurs; you had to have your boots shined. I think I was getting ninety-five pounds a week to work there. It was basically slave labor. Most of the people working there were young like me, because when they got older they had the sense to leave. He'd get all these little apprentices, like me, and promise them rides in races, but never let them ride anything for him.

It's awful over there [in England] for a woman trying to be a jockey. You've either got to be married to somebody, or have some money...there's only a few women riders, and they're pretty well connected. They're both steeplechase and flat riders. But the money sucks, because they never get many rides.

I was with Sir Mark for almost two years. Then I decided I wanted to come to America, because I thought, "Well, I can be a jockey in America."

An assistant trainer to Sir Mark had ridden some steeplechase races for Michael Dickinson when Dickinson was still in England. *(Editors' note: Dickinson was a successful trainer in England before coming to America in 1987, where his numerous stakes winners have included Da Hoss, two-time winner of the Breeders' Cup Mile.)* He suggested I write Michael a letter, and he wrote me back and said, "Sure, come on over." So I hopped on a plane and landed in Columbia, South Carolina. I was nineteen. I've been here [in the United States] ever since.

I didn't have a clue about American racing. Michael used to like to pull us into the house and have little lessons in all the various

American racing comments and phrases. I mean, I had never heard the expression "breezing"; we just worked our horses in England. Michael would give us little tests.

Michael taught us how to read the *Daily Racing Form*. We never paid any attention to [horses'] times in England. He taught me about that. He used to put these little headphones on us during the workouts, and he'd say, "You're going too slow," or "too fast," or "How fast do you think you were going?" We'd have to guess how fast we went. When I first came over, someone might say to me, "Go in :36," and I might go out and work the horse two miles. I had no idea what was going on (laughs). I said my math wasn't very good. But I learned. You just practice, and you pick it up. It's important.

I was fortunate that I never rode in England and learned the English style of race riding, because I've seen a lot of English guys come over and work for Michael, and Michael is very big on the American style of racing. He used to watch us and tell us, "Get down a bit lower."

I rode my first (unofficial) race in America for Michael at Charlotte, North Carolina, in a point-to-point race. It was pissing down rain; it was horrible. But I won. It wasn't a pari-mutuel race. The horse's name was They Call Me Charlie. It was great.

Michael knew I wanted to be a jockey. He was trying to help me every way he could. When I left him, he gave me the names of a bunch of people. He thought I should go straight to Atlantic City (racetrack) and start riding there. But I wasn't fully legal then (from a citizenship status), so I had to be careful. I didn't want to stop once I started. You don't want to piss somebody off and have them call immigration. Also, I didn't think I was quite ready yet. I didn't know enough. I wasn't strong enough. There were a lot of women galloping horses or breaking them, but not many were riding races. I would have looked all right on a horse until the race started, then I would have looked like a pack of shit.

After I left Michael, I went to work for another English trainer, Chris Speckert. I stayed with him for almost three years. I worked for him at Keeneland and went with him to New Orleans that first year. They have a bunch of training races at the Fair Grounds there. So that was great for me — I got to ride loads and loads of training races. It was a wonderful experience.

After about three years, I left Chris and went to work for Mike Stidham at the Fair Grounds. I rode schooling races then, too. He was going to Arlington last summer (2000). I'd been to Arlington to visit some friends of mine three years before. I thought, "My God, this place is awesome." So I went with Mike. I was going to start riding there; my immigration papers had all gotten sorted out.

I was thinking, "I've got to do this right." I wanted to wait till the right time. I didn't want to look like a sap. There's nothing wrong with just galloping horses [for a living], but I don't want to be doing that when I'm forty. I wanted to go into riding so I could make more money and retire when I wanted to. It would give me independence. Mike Stidham was onto me, asking, "When are you going to start?" And, "What are you waiting for? I want to put you on your first horse."

I'd go and gallop some horses for Mike real early every morning; then I'd go around with the guy I'd hired to be my agent, Bobby Kelly. He worked as an assistant trainer to Louis Roussel for number of years. He's a real hustler, and he knows a lot of people. So, Bobby and I would hit the barns. I knew I couldn't depend on only Mike to give me mounts. I had to make some money from other people, too.

Mike Stidham's assistant, Hillary Pridham, had some horses in the barn as well. She had a little filly I'd been working named Prize and Joy. So we decided I'd ride her. The filly is entered, and there I am in the track program.

I was a little nervous in the morning, and then I'm like, "[Expletive] it, if something goes wrong; it's not my fault. It's my first ride. They can't blame me." Arlington is such a great place...the people were all out...it was a big crowd — it was Belmont Stakes Day. The place was packed. I thought, like, "Wow, this is great."

We go in the gate; that was no problem. I was like, "Lah dah." I was relaxed. Mike had said, "Just come with a run down the lane." The filly was not the favorite. There were only six horses in the race.

So we broke, and I think (Hall of Fame jockey) Earlie Fires went off to the lead. After him there was no one in front of me, so I was just going along down the backside, and Earlie's horse is way in front of me. I'd come out of the gate, and I hadn't fallen off, and there's only five other horses in the race, so I'm thinking, "How bad can it be?"

When we get to about the half-mile pole, I'm starting to catch up to Earlie. When we get to the quarter pole, I'm thinking, "Now we're *really* starting to catch him up. Oh, shit, I better start *doing* something!…Well, [expletive], I'm going to catch Earlie Fires!" And the next thing I know we've crossed the wire in front.

I was more astounded than anything. I was more in shock. I'd won the first (pari-mutuel) race that I'd ever been in. And of course I come back and everyone's screaming and cheering. And Christine Gabriel interviewed me (on Arlington's in-house television). All I thought was, "I just want to go and have a beer now, thank you."

When I first came to Chicago, a lot of people said, "Oh, you girls never make it here. It's really hard." I think winning my first race helped a lot. People sat up and said, "Well, you know what? She's actually all right."

Things started picking up almost right away. But it wasn't all smooth. The next day I rode one for (trainer) Pat Cuccurullo. It was a horrible day. It was pissing down rain. The track was sloppy — I'd never ridden on a sloppy track before — so, of course, I dropped my whip in the gate. I called out to the starter, "Hold on, I've dropped my whip." And all the other jocks are mimicking me, saying "Oh, I've dropped my whip. I've dropped my whip." I said, "Shut up before I smack you." And I ran last.

When I went to use my whip, it was brutal. In all the years I'd worked horses, I'd never used a whip. Everybody said, "Zoe, you looked great until you picked up that whip." [Jockey] Mark Guidry said to me, "Zoe, you're doing really good, but just don't hit 'em until you can hit 'em better."

But I practiced a lot to get better. It took me a good while for me to be comfortable with the whip. At first, I used to look back to see where I was whipping. Somebody said, "Zoe, you don't have to look — that part of the horse isn't going anywhere." Which made sense.

The other jockeys were helpful. There were two other girls here then, Mary Jo Brennan and Kelly Sampson, and they were great to me, and so were the guys. Listening to guys like Ray Sibille and Carlos Silva and Earlie Fires helped me improve. Even now, one of them might pull me aside and say, "What the hell were you doing out there? It won't cut it if you do something that winds up dropping everyone else." So I do a lot of listening and learning.

Now I'm the only woman riding here in Chicago. But I'm not isolated. I'm only in my own little (jockey) room when I'm getting changed or having a shower. Because we all hang out in the track kitchen anyway, or else I'm in the exercise room. I just kind of consider myself one of the lads here, so to speak. That's fine. I wouldn't care if there never was another girl rider here.

✤✤✤✤✤

Getting mounts is never easy. There was one trainer who always rode the bug (used apprentice jockeys on his horses), but he would *never* use me. Bobby and I would stop there every day at his barn, and he was always very nice, but he would never use me.

I've got the gift of gab, especially with some of the older trainers. I just like to mix with them. The things that come out of my mouth might actually not be too ladylike. But maybe that actually helps sometimes. They might laugh and think, "Well, she's not a typical girl rider."

There have been good girl riders who didn't have an opportunity to get on good horses. I don't think it's a matter of strength. You get strong finishers and weak finishers in men riders, too. Some people have natural ability; horses just run for them; strength doesn't matter. Look at Pat Day. I can't say he's a strong finisher, but he judges them so well that he goes flying by them anyway. I'd love to nail him on the wire (laughs).

I work hard. You've got to. You've got to go around to the barns. Not everyone does. When I work horses in the mornings, I stand out because I wear red-red pants, red jacket, red cap. They call me "la niña roja" (the red girl).

In England, for Sir Mark Prescott, we had to wear basic black britches and brown and yellow caps. Disgusting. So when I came to America and saw everyone wore jeans, I said, "This is cool." I had some red jeans and decided I would wear them one day. Another day I wore a red jacket, too. I've got a cupboard full of red clothes.

When I first went to Kentucky, I'd wear that outfit in the mornings. And people would say, "Who's the girl in red?" So it became a bit of a trademark. They can't miss me, that's for sure. Of course, sometimes that's not such a good thing." (laughs)

Weight has not been a big concern to me. I weighed 120 when I was getting ready to ride, so I went on a diet. It was called "don't eat." I got really light; I was tacking 106 then. I've never been skinny. I'm five foot. I've always had policewoman's ankles.

I never lost strength. I was running every day — I still do, a couple of miles. I get on the skiing machine. I don't lift weights — I'm too muscular already. Me and Ray Sibille are the only ones in the jocks' exercise room everyday. Ray's in great shape, and he's like forty-eight and still riding great.

I watch everything I eat. Breakfast is coffee. I kind of live on a diet of Power Bars and Red Bull (an energy drink). So I really don't eat much during the day, and I'll have a salad at night. I'm vegetarian anyway. My big letdown is beer and chocolates, unfortunately. Everybody has something.

I'd rather be a pound overweight than go and sit in the hot box for four hours and get really weak. And I don't want to get to the point where I have to flip (intentionally vomit to lose weight). A lot of guys do that. I won't do that. I'd rather not eat than do that.

I've broken tons of stuff — my leg when I was seven; fell off my pony Mischief who'd run off with me. I was in traction for seven weeks. I've broken my arms, nose, ribs. When I worked for Michael (Dickinson), I went through a fence with a horse and lacerated my liver. That put me out for a while. I was in the hospital for only three days, but it was awful — I couldn't drink for six months.

When I got hurt at Arlington last summer, I was out of action for six weeks. I didn't really even think I broke anything at the time. It happened behind the gate. Horse reared up and ran backwards and then fell on top of me. I got a fractured pubic bone — you could say I broke my box. It happened so quickly. I really wasn't feeling any pain as I laid there — more just a numbness.

Then the horse was loose, and he was flying around the track going the wrong way before he turned around and started to come back toward the gate. It was the last race of the day. So I look up and he's coming right for us. I'm on a stretcher, and they've got me held down with duct tape, which I wasn't too pleased with. And the ambulance guys said, "Oh, shit, here comes that horse. We've got to move her quick." But then somebody diverted the horse and he went back around again without running over me before they caught him.

It made me realize that maybe I had taken stuff a bit for granted, that maybe bad stuff can happen. It made me sit up and appreciate how lucky I'd been to have such a good start.

My dad gets the races from here on his computer in England. And Mum's getting, like, able to read the *Form* now. She looks at the past performances of some of the horses I ride, and she gets puzzled. She asks me, "What does this mean at the end of the horse's line where it says 'Tired.' Why are your horses tired all the time?" Or she's noticed that it says maybe the horse closed "belatedly." She's like, "Why are they always belated?"

Now that my dad has become such a racing buff, he said to me: "I've read that after your lose your bug (apprentice allowance) nobody's going to want you. So we'd better come over to see you in July so we can see you ride."

Actually, I'm not nervous about losing the bug. It's going to happen. You want it to happen when you're on a good streak and winning. If it happens when you're in a slump, it might really suck.

I mind getting beat, but as long as I've done everything I could do, and the horse has done everything it could do, that's all you can ask. I'd rather ride a poor old horse with three good legs that tries than a horse with four good legs that doesn't try.

I haven't had any huge slump yet in my career. I went like a week one time when I didn't win a race, and I got down. But I realized that when you're down, you don't ride as good.

So, I don't cry in the shower. Tomorrow's another day.

M A R Y J E A N   W A L L

$\mathcal{T}$he Write Stuff

$\mathcal{M}$aryjean Wall realized early in her life that she wanted to participate in Thoroughbred horse racing. The question facing her was: In what capacity?

After rejecting notions of becoming a jockey or a trainer, goals she deemed "unrealistic" at the time, Wall began a determined attempt to enter the ranks of racing journalists.

This vocational choice eventually rewarded the Windsor, Ontario, native with a fulfilling career highlighted by numerous professional achievements. Since she began covering racing for the Lexington Herald-Leader in 1973 (the paper was the Lexington Herald at the time), Wall has won Eclipse Awards for newspaper writing — one in 1980, 1997, and 1999. She was the first female winner of that award, and with her most recent Eclipse, she became only the second journalist to win three Eclipses.

Wall is also a three-time winner of the John Hervey Award, for writing on harness racing. In 1991, she won the Associated Press

*Sports Editors' best sports story for her coverage of the Belmont
Stakes. And in 1999, the Kentucky Thoroughbred Owners and
Breeders honored her with the Engelhard Award, which is given to a
member of the media for his or her outstanding service to the
Thoroughbred industry.*

*For years, the Lexington resident has competed her Arabian hors-
es. Her other interests include visiting racetracks in odd places, gar-
dening, canoeing, and camping.*

I moved to Kentucky as a teenager because I wanted to be in
horse country. As far as racehorses are concerned, I think I
was about twelve years old when I read *The Black Stallion*.
I'm another alumnus of the (author) Walter Farley school of influence. If I had a dollar for every person I've interviewed in my career
who got into racing because of reading *The Black Stallion*, I'd have
my retirement plan in great shape.

I have a bachelor's degree in history from the University of
Kentucky. My plan all along was to get into journalism at the university, but I was putting myself through school, paying all my own
bills, and I wasn't happy with the journalism program at that time.
I also had an intense love of history, so I switched to that because I
wanted to get my money's worth. This was American history,
although I did take a course in Canadian history. I have been doing
graduate work in American history, which I find to be fascinating.

I was born in a suburb of Windsor. I used to ride my bike five

Maryjean Wall has chronicled many of the sport's great horses and people.

miles each way to go to work at a riding stable that was run by a woman named Violet Hopkins. I didn't realize it at the time, but learned later that she was renowned as a dressage trainer and teacher. She gave us some wonderful foundations in dressage riding. I used to work for my lessons. I was unbelievably lucky to have her as a teacher.

No one in my family liked horses. No one was very supportive of my horse venture, although my mother bought me my first pair of riding pants — they were used — and my father used to drive me out to the stable in the winter when I couldn't ride my bike there. That's about as far as their support went. I am sure that they were appalled when I started getting interested in horse racing and announced that I was going to work in it. I can remember my mother saying, "If you like horses, the only way you're ever going to get to be around them is to become a secretary for someone on a ranch, or marry someone on a ranch."

I was the oldest child. My mother did not graduate from high school, but that was not her fault. She had to quit school to help support her brother going to college. My father was a salesman.

My family had emigrated to Canada only one generation earlier. My grandfather came first to Buffalo. He came from Wales, but he was Irish; we're all Irish. I guess they left Ireland and went to Wales during the potato famine in Ireland. I'm told my grandfather learned English in a speller he would read while riding the bus to work every day. Somehow he ended up in Canada and was a very successful businessman. Our family owned the factory that canned all the vegetables for the Green Giant Company in Canada.

But a lot happened to the family's money. By the time my grandfather died, we no longer had the factory; it had been sold and was publicly held. My father was losing his job with that company, where he had represented the family's interests. I was a teenager. I

Wall in the show ring on a favorite horse.

was aware that it was a very tough time for my parents. My dad had decided to move everybody to Florida because he could support them better there. I went briefly to Florida with them, all the while with the intention of coming up to Kentucky to go to college, but by that time they couldn't afford to pay for my education.

So, I went to secretarial school and then worked as a secretary for a year to save money to pay for my first year of college. I worked the whole time I was going to college. I worked at the *Lexington Herald-Leader*. I would work partly in the afternoon and partly at night; then I'd go to classes in the mornings. I took eight years to get my degree. But I gained a lot of newspaper experience during that time.

The idea of me becoming a journalist was all tied to the horses. Soon after I got interested in the racehorses, I thought, "Oh, I want to work with them all my life. That's what I want to do." But I didn't know what to do.

I knew I couldn't be a jockey, because women couldn't be jockeys then. Here I was riding for years, but that door was closed to me. I never thought of challenging it. The Civil Rights Act hadn't been passed yet to disallow gender discrimination. So, that door was just completely closed. And I had no concept of becoming a trainer — that was not an idea that I could grasp at the time. So, I decided that I would write about racehorses — which was about as farfetched as being a jockey, but not quite.

In Windsor, I found it hard to make the leap (from the riding stable to the racetrack). It took a long time. I didn't know how to get to the racetrack. I knew about them from Walter Farley's books, and I used to take a bus downtown to buy a copy of *Turf & Sport Digest*. There was one newsstand in Windsor where you could buy it. I remember the first copy I ever bought had a picture of Bally Ache winning the Preakness the previous year. That was in the early sixties, and there was another Preakness coming up, so I watched it on TV, and I was hooked. But I still didn't know how to get to the racetrack.

Detroit Race Course is across the river from Windsor. I managed to talk my mother into accompanying me to the races at Detroit one afternoon. I think that the deal was, if I had been a good girl all year or something like that — that was the only way she would let me go to the track. She said, "You must go with an adult." She did not think highly of the racetrack at all. So, bless her heart, because it must have been a sacrifice for her, the two of us took the bus from Windsor to Detroit. We thought we could then take another bus to the racetrack. I had investigated all this. But it turned out you had to take a cab. And you know what was sitting in the cab we took? Some cigar-smoking gamblers with their noses in the *Racing Form*. I was in hog heaven. "My gosh," I thought, "there are people who really do read this paper!" My mother must have been dying.

Some years later I would sneak off to the races at Woodbine. I'd tell my mother I'd been shopping. So I learned how to get to the track as a spectator, but I didn't know how to get a job there. I can remember calling the Michigan Racing Commission one time to ask them how to get a job at the track. They told me I could stand outside the track and hope that a trainer might invite me in. This was at Detroit — I mean, like, come on! There was nothing else in place in racing at that time that I knew of to help an outsider like me who wanted to get in the game. It began to look more and more like the only way I was going to be able to get in would be through getting an education, go in through that door.

But even after I got the education and had been working at the paper (*Herald-Leader*) a long time, there was no prospect of a Turf writing job opening up. I waited six years before an opportunity happened. I was working as a reporter, and didn't like working as a reporter, and might even have been getting close to quitting. I didn't find any great joy in going to the courthouse every day. Then the person that was doing the racing writing told me that he was probably going to quit. He said, "Just be ready." And one day he came by my desk — he'd just stormed out of the editor's office; he'd quit — and he said, "Go apply for the job." And I did. It took them a while to decide to hire me, but to their credit they gave the job to me. The paper was then the *Lexington Herald*. Women just weren't doing that work then.

This was Secretariat's three-year-old year (1973). No other

women were then doing this work as a daily beat for a newspaper that I know about. Jobie Arnold had written for newspapers, and so had Mary Jane Gallaher. (Arnold also wrote for magazines and was the first female handicapper. Gallaher wrote a column for the *Lexington Leader* and for racing magazines.) I was always told that Jobie's stuff was more about social notes at the racetrack — I don't know this as a fact — and that Mary Jane might have written more about the horses. I remember reading a story about Jobie Arnold in *Turf & Sport Digest* when I was a teenager. It showed a photo of her in the press box. I remember her talking in the story about going through the clubhouse every day to see who was having lunch. Nevertheless, she was a woman in the press box. And I found that to be very inspirational.

The job was year-round. I focused on how I had envisioned it. So I crafted or fashioned my own way of doing it, which consisted of going to the barns every morning and hanging out as much as I could with the horsemen year-round, not just during the race meetings. And doing other little things, like combing the *Racing Form* for clues as to stories to write about. You almost had to be creative, calling people on the phone, trying to build connections at the track.

When I started, I had no mentors. I can't tell you how awful it was and how scared I was. Going into press boxes where I had to fight my way in, at least at first. And the barn areas, where I knew absolutely no one. Some people openly despised me. There was one prominent trainer who would never ever speak to me. It was a hard burden to shoulder. I don't know why he didn't like me. But when you're young, it's hard to walk up to somebody like that and say, "Hey, you S.O.B., why won't you talk to me?"

It was hard to get people to talk to me. I don't know if it was because I was young, because I was a woman, because I walked in there not knowing anybody — it was probably all three. Later, I realized that it wasn't just me — that they just didn't want a woman around.

The women's movement was in the sixties and seventies. I remember it being there, but at the time I never got involved in it because I was working so hard, working full time, and going to school, too. I was aware of them out there fighting their fight, but I had no dog in that fight. I was just trying to survive. And once I got my writing job, I was just so happy that I was getting to do the work I wanted to do that I wasn't looking at it from the standpoint of, "Oh, I'm a woman breaking new ground." Once I got into the job, I was so engrossed in trying to be a better writer all the time — that was always the foremost thing in my mind — that I didn't sit around and think, "Oh, there are roadblocks because I am a woman."

You had to have a certain way of skipping around things in order to function back then. There was another trainer; he trained an extremely high-profile horse in the 1970s. When he came through Kentucky, I had absolutely no rapport with him in person. But I found out that on the phone, he would talk to me. So that's what I did. It was amazing. It made me feel small a lot of times. But there was nothing I could do about it except persevere.

You knew you weren't going into the jockeys' room (for interviews). It didn't make a bit of difference to me. All the men thought they had to go in there, and they did. I didn't see why you had to — you could talk to the jockeys in the mornings, or you could talk to them when they got off their horses after races. Why did you have to go in the showers with them?

A couple of times this did become an issue. I remember at Keeneland it became an issue one year when Bill Shoemaker came there to ride in a stakes, and, of course, all the men were going into the jockeys' room to talk to him. Recently, I found a letter that the *Herald* wrote to Keeneland, explaining to them that they couldn't let just men only in the jockeys' room. After that, the way it worked at Keeneland was instead of letting me in, nobody would go in. Now, we can all talk to the jockeys in another room. When the letter was sent, it wasn't because I wanted to go into the jockeys' room. It was just that I wanted access to the jockey like everybody else.

I've since been in jockeys' rooms. When they first started letting women in, it was a badge of honor; I mean, you had to go in. The tracks were finally bending over backwards to be fair to us.

The men writers were always very accepting of me. Pete Axthelm, Sam McCracken, Red Smith — they were all really nice to me. Pete would talk to me about writing. Red was always complimentary and encouraging. It made me feel accepted; it made me feel good.

I was proposed for membership in the National Turf Writers

Association. No woman had ever been accepted. It took them a long time to vote on me. I was told that members said, "We can't have this," but they were told that they had to. It was about a year after being proposed that I was accepted. To come from nowhere and finally get in the National Turf Writers made me feel very good, very proud. And I eventually served three terms as a (NTWA) director.

The thing I always felt was that I had to work triple hard to prove myself. I used to read all the good sportswriters so that I could learn from them. Writing was hard for me, and it is still hard for me, and I worked very, very hard at it. I was aware at the time that I was working harder than the men. But I didn't feel that that was only because I was a woman — I felt it was because I was in a small market, and people didn't take a small market as seriously. I wanted a national name. So I would freelance for magazines. I thought, "If they're not going to read me in the *Herald*, and there was no Internet then, the only way that I could become nationally known was to write for national publications. It was a lot of extra work.

When I won my first Eclipse Award, even though I felt I had done some good work by then, I couldn't believe it. I remember the work I put into getting the first one, which now pales before the work I put in getting my second and third Eclipse Awards. I mean the field is so much more competitive now. To be recognized that way was beyond any dream I'd had.

Over the years the things that I've enjoyed most writing about are the characters on the racetrack. They live in a way and do things in a way that probably no other culture does in America. I mean, I once wrote a story about a guy, an old black groom, who had a special recipe for cooking up a groundhog stew in the tack room where he lived. He gave me his recipe and I published it in the paper. It had things in it like the red pepper that is used in horse bandages. And he said if it were a real special groundhog, he would drive it to town and cook it on somebody's stove. But he emphasized, "I will never eat a possum." He drew the line there.

I love that kind of thing. Think about how many people go to work every day; they just trudge off. They look at the same boring people every day. They watch the clock. I know because I did that for a year when I worked as a secretary. That's not my cup of tea. I just love to walk out to the racetrack in the morning and find out who might be cooking a groundhog stew. Or who might be getting married in the receiving barn. I went to a wedding in the receiving barn at old Latonia years ago.

I spent a lot of time in (Hall of Fame trainer) Woody Stephens' barn. I did it on my vacations. I would go up to Saratoga on my vacations. There are some interesting observations about this. When I first started doing it, and that would be in the mid-1970s, Turf writers didn't seem to go to the barns up there. Now, of course, they do. I would be in Woody's stable every morning and nary a Turf writer would come around, even though Woody by then had won the Kentucky Derby.

This tells you the changes, how competitive Turf writing has become. You know that Woody would be pestered to death now. In fact, as time went on, Woody was pestered to death, but they hadn't discovered him then, which amazed me because he had been such a successful trainer in New York for years. The New York bettors certainly knew him.

I was around some tremendous horses in those years. This was Woody's heyday, and he had Cannonade, who won the Derby (1974), and some really fantastic fillies and mares. I guess they were mainly fillies. He had De La Rose, Heavenly Cause; oh, there were tons of them.

Woody was demanding because he expected you to handle a horse. But he also assumed that anyone coming up from Kentucky knew how to handle horses. His barn was full of Kentucky people. They knew where to go to look for work when they got to New York.

For Woody you were walking really valuable horses. I learned to put bandages on a horse — it was a Round Table filly. That was a real mark of honor for me; I didn't learn on some old claiming horse (laughs). I learned because I would go to the barn in the afternoon and work with bandages. Somebody in the barn showed me how to do it. Actually, I learned about every phase of stable operation then. This was very valuable to me in my job.

Mrs. John A. Morris (long a prominent owner of Thoroughbreds) was still alive then. She was one of Woody's regular clients, and she'd come around the barn in the morning. Now, this is just a touch of old Saratoga: Mrs. Morris would wear gloves up to her elbows. And she and Woody would go and buy clover off a truck every morning — fresh clover — and she would feed it to her horses in her long gloves. And I thought that was beautiful.

There is a problem in that the racing game has gone so much more to business. And so many old-time horsemen have disappeared. That's where I notice changes, and I don't like them.

It really hit home with me when I interviewed David Vance (trainer of Caressing, the 2000 Eclipse Award-winning two-year-old filly) for a profile last fall.

David is an old-time horseman. Everything we talked about, stories about horses he used to train, how he would keep them racing, how he would mix his own leg paints — I was so conscious that this was what it was like twenty years ago all the time when I interviewed people. But I don't hear those stories anymore.

I really respect David for his knowledge of horses, the sense of the past that he gave. He is a character. It was great to see him win the Breeders' Cup (Juvenile Fillies) with Caressing. If anyone would deserve that, it would be a person like him who has given his whole life to the game.

And David came up the old way, by the seat of his pants. And he survived. You don't find many people like that anymore. You find little businessmen running these barns. Some of them may be good horsemen, others might not, but they're businessmen. They're not the characters we had in the old days. Today, these people would die before they would want to be seen as a character. In the old days, people reveled in that.

I don't know how I got started seeking out racetracks. I "collect" visits to racetracks the way some people build lifetime lists of visits to ballparks, or sightings of birds.

I'm not the only one doing it. I have maybe right around sixty tracks, but I've been told I'm just a piker in that area. There's a couple in Maryland, Bob and Beverly Beck; they're probably the champs. They've probably been to two-hundred tracks.

At one time I would go intentionally seeking tracks. Now, it's just if there happens to be one in the area that I haven't been to, I'll go there. Having said that, I must admit I did make a trip to Montana last summer to one of the Crow Indian reservations to see their races. So I guess I'm still at it.

The races on the Crow reservation were pretty neat. Those were among the best-looking horses I've ever seen at a bush track. They were all well fed, shiny, and there was not a lame horse among them. It wasn't what you would picture at an off-the-wall place. There was a plain little concrete grandstand. But it was a nice enough racing strip — it wasn't a plowed field or anything — and there was a rodeo going in the infield at the same time as the races. It was an all-Indian rodeo, but anybody could participate in the horse races. The races were both for Quarter Horses and Thoroughbreds. They had some Shetland ponies doing relay races. All kinds of things. I had a great time out there.

Some of the best places I've been I did not go to specifically looking for racing. I found a track on Prince Edward Island (Canada).
We were talking to the locals and they were telling us about this
racetrack. Now, this is not Charlotte Town Driving Park, or whatever it's called; that's the renowned harness track on (Prince
Edward Island) where some of the most famous drivers in history
have come from. No, this track was out at the other end of the
island. It had some kind of official name, but the locals called it the
"Track for Older Horses and Older Men." The best stories in the
world come from places like this or Cajun Downs in Louisiana,
places so small they don't even have mutuel machines.

I grew up not far from old Kenilworth Park in Windsor. That was
the course where Man o' War ran his last race, beating Triple Crown
winner Sir Barton in their famous match race, October 12, 1920.

I think I was twelve when I first took riding lessons at
Kenilworth. The track was long closed, but you could rent livery
stable horses there. There was one barn left, I guess left over from
the racetrack days. It cost two dollars an hour to rent a horse. I can
remember this because I got twenty-five cents a week in allowance,
and I would save my money for two months in order to get the two
dollars to ride the horse for an hour.

The horse I always rode was named Pearl. I always rented her.
Pearl ran off with me one day and gave me a fit. She ran off down
a section of the old racetrack that Man o' War had run over. I was

always aware that Man o' War had raced there, and it was right in the front of my mind that Pearl and I were on hallowed ground. Maybe I wasn't thinking that at the moment that Pearl was running off with me — I was scared for my life — but I remember talking about it later: "Oh, yeah, I got run off with by Pearl on the track where Man o' War last raced." I would tell people that.

I've been back there many times looking for Kenilworth Park. You can't find it now; it's all houses. But I know where it was. It's like going to a shrine.

CHAPTER 16

DOT SIBILLE

*T*he Relationship

W*hen Dot Johnson witnessed her first match race at age ten, she got hooked on the sport. This took place deep in the heart of Cajun country, a small region of Louisiana that has produced more riding talent per acre than any other area in the world. It is there that match races provide prime weekend recreation for horse-loving residents, serving also as the first testing ground for young boys learning the art of race riding. Match races are unsanctioned contests at unrecognized tracks and betting is done man to man or through on-track bookmakers.*

She made many subsequent visits to the bush tracks, then some years later a fateful trip to Evangeline Downs in Lafayette, where she first caught sight of her future husband. His name was Ray Sibille, and he and Dot married in 1971. A native of Sunset, Louisiana, Ray had graduated from the match-race world to pari-mutuel tracks, becoming a member of a Cajun riding roster that includes stars such as Eddie Delahoussaye, Randy Romero, Shane Sellers, Kent Desormeaux, Mark Guidry, and

Robby Albarado. Through 2000 Ray Sibille had won more than four-thousand races and ridden hundreds of stakes winners, major among them Great Communicator, hero of the 1988 Breeders' Cup Turf.

Throughout their marriage, Dot Sibille has wanted to be right there at the racetrack with her husband. Consequently, over the years she has worked as a workout spotter, switchboard operator, and, most recently, as a clocker at the Chicago tracks. She has also teamed with Ray, a director of the Jockeys' Guild, to help provide direction to several racing charities, including the Don MacBeth Memorial Fund, which assists disabled riders. Dot Sibille has thus gained a perspective on the sport from two standpoints: that of paid participant and as the wife of one of those few professional athletes who go to work several times a day with an ambulance following behind them.

Our family is from a Louisiana bayou town called Cecilia. It's about eight miles from the crawfish capital of the world, Breaux Bridge, Louisiana.

But I was raised more out of Louisiana than in it. My dad was in construction and we traveled a lot. We lived a lot in Florida, Mississippi, and Texas. But we still have land in Louisiana and family there. I have two sisters who are still there, in the same little town, Cecilia. There are five of us kids, all girls.

We went to the match races with our aunt, my mom's sister, to watch our cousin ride. That's Henry Lee Patin, whose sister Tina is married to

Throughout her marriage, Dot Sibille has been right there at the racetrack with her husband, Ray.

(jockey) Mark Guidry. At the time, Ray would go and ride the match races, too. But we never met up with him.

They had match races all over, but the one we would go to was right by my aunt's house. It was called Patin's racetrack, and it was a straightaway. They had what they'd call "arpents" — which are sprints. They'd break them out of the gate, and some of the horses just had beer cans on their backs. And my little cousin he'd get up there with just his bathing suit on, no boots, no nothing, and they'd just go. It was the funnest, especially Saturday and Sundays. And they had the best barbeque pork sandwiches ever!

People would come from surrounding communities, Arnaudville, or wherever they had little racetracks and guys raising Quarter Horses in their back yards. And they'd watch the kids.

All these guys, Larry Melancon, Ray, Kent Desormeaux, Mark Guidry, a bunch of them — if you look across the country at the top five riders, one of them will be from Louisiana. I think it's because they started so young. They had the horses right there at the house, and they had their own barn. They learned to ride in the pastures. Some of them, they came out of diapers and were on the horses.

The boys eventually started going to the bigger racetracks. But these guys were all people we originally knew from the town.

I'll never forget this big black horse had a swayback, and my cousin was so small, they'd put a pillow and then a saddle on the horse. He was that deep and his name was Swayback and he won so many races!

And they had another named Cher Gris, that means Gray Tail in French. That's another thing, you hardly ever spoke English around there; it was all the French people. I remember thinking it was the greatest thing on earth — *and* you can bet on them!

I was about seventeen when I met Ray and he was riding at Evangeline (Downs in Lafayette, Louisiana). He was nineteen. I met him through my cousin, Henry Lee Patin. We got married about six months after we met. We've been married twenty-nine years.

I'm not saying anything about any other jocks' wives, or any-thing…but I was always asking questions. I've always just loved it. Every year we go back for the Jockeys' Guild Convention in Vegas, and the wives always go like a day or two before. And it's like a reunion with my sister and all of us. (Dot's sister Sheila married jockey Pat Day in 1979.) Well, all these girls, they can't wait to go shopping. But I do not leave the racebook (a simulcast parlor inside a casino) 'til the last race is over.

And then there's nothing more beautiful than at five o'clock in the morning when the sun's coming up and you see horses coming around the turn. It's the best time of the day for me. And a lot of the wives say, "How do you get up at 4:30 in the morning?" I say, "If you'd be out there when those babies start off, you know, we might be looking at a Triple Crown horse right here." You just never know, and that's the thrill.

I bet. Ray, most of the time, he's asking me, "What do you think of this horse?" I'll say, "Well, I think you just worked a good two-year-old and you ought to go by that barn." Stuff like that. But when we get together, Ray and I, especially for the Breeders' Cup, that is the best thing in the world. It's the best horse-racing day because you get them all together to handicap. When you can say, "Oh, man, I picked that horse out of the best horses in the country" — that is the greatest reward!

Like I tell Ray, my fantasy, I guess, would be to ride in a race. But I'm afraid of horses when I'm around them. Because I respect them. [The horse is] not gonna kick me in the face because I know he'll do that in a second, you know?

There was a time when my son, Keary, was in first or second grade and a friend of mine, Sally Arroyo, we rode jumpers. And it was nice and everything. But it wasn't that speed and that excitement — you know? So an equestrian rider I'm not. Maybe it would only take one time for me to ride in a race and see how scary it is. I often think about it. And now with the little TV cameras they have on the rider's helmet, I'll think, "Oh, that's pretty close to being in the race."

When our son was small, I thought my thing was to be the mother — which it was. But when Ray'd come home, I was always interested in what happened at the racetrack. I wouldn't miss a chance to go the racetrack, and Keary loved coming out here when he was younger. So I was always out here.

Ray is not a stressful kind of person...bringing something that was bad at the racetrack home. He would cut it off at a point and that was it. We always talk about the good things, the interesting things. We do everything together. I guess it stems back from my mother and father. I mean, like she always told me, "I know we travel, but you will learn — if you really want to learn, you will learn at this place, 'cause I'm going to be with your dad." And that's the way they were; they did everything together.

You know, I've been around other people who…well, God knows how much I hated Pat Day when he was in drugs and my sister was too. I was there. And I've seen some guys too that I didn't think were on drugs and the way they'd come back and talk to their wives. But the upbringing and the respect that Ray has for people, and women in general, that's just his personality. His mom and dad were the greatest people on earth, I think. He treats people the way he wants to be treated. And that's the way my mom and dad were, too.

I don't think there's a hard thing about being a rider's wife. And now Pat and Sheila are just great because they've been sober and off stuff for years. And the best thing that ever happened to them was when they were able to adopt Irene. They got her when she was two days old. That's their life. 'Cause like when Sheila and Irene come over here and they'll spend the night at the house, Pat's on the phone to Sheila. "Where's my baby girl?" And like he says, "My baby girl, I can't hold her anymore!" — that's their life. And they've got a great life now, thank goodness. I now have more respect for this guy than a lot of men in this world.

But we have a different thing, Ray and I do. I don't think there's anything bad about being a rider's wife. Girls who cut my hair say, "That's got to be exciting." And I say, "It is!" What wife can go to their husband's job and watch them and be excited at the same time? I mean there's not too many women that say "I can go watch my husband at work." What, sit at a desk? Maybe that's what they like. But for me, every minute that I watch my husband is exciting. So I think it's a privilege to be a rider's wife.

I guess it's because we've always been so fortunate — knock on wood. Ray has had injuries, but nothing we couldn't overcome. But I've seen other riders, you know they come every year, the quadriplegics that have happened on the track and all that. Ray's on his thirty-first year of riding, and we've just been so fortunate.

That's why I do these (racetrack) charities. I guess that feeling of giving something back. Like (young Chicago jockey) Joel Campbell starting off, and he and his girlfriend just had the baby. He's had a broken pelvis. It's been months now, you know?

We need to raise money so we can take care of all these hurt riders, and we're not only talking about jockeys that get hurt. Like say an exercise rider, he has family that lives in the backside. These exercise riders get hurt too. We're there to help them, if they need, God forbid, a wheelchair or something. It's disabled riders. It's not only exclusive for jockeys.

I'm a chicken for pain, but Ray has a very high tolerance of pain. He's had the collarbone broken three times and had surgery in one of them and put a pin in. But the scaredest I ever got was in San Francisco. He came out of the gate and a filly mashed his lower abdomen. He was worried about a hole or something they had to stitch up.

Well, we're at this hospital in San Francisco. Usually in the emergency room they don't tend to pay attention as much as that. But there was this one emergency doctor, and she says, "Look at the bottom of his foot." I came to the end of the bed and one foot was kind of purple. She says, "There's no circulation there." So she called in a vascular surgeon. Ray says, "No, stitch me up. I'm okay. We're going to go to dinner."

They rush him into surgery. We had to wait about an hour for him. And he had to have a six-inch artificial artery put in where the horse had mashed him. And he could have lost his leg that night.

But when they first go down — anybody that's going that speed, naturally you get the wind knocked out of you totally. And all you want to do is see them move...and they can't move at that point. They're just trying to catch their breath out there. And after that, they get up, and you know they are some tough cookies. They naturally learn to roll, so as long as that horse clears him...

It's that scariness, but then all of the sudden you forget about it. That may sound weird, but if every time the gate opened I thought, "Oh my goodness, Ray..." I couldn't even like the sport. Accidents happen sometimes and hopefully they're okay. But then the next race is on, let's go, you know? So when Ray was out with broken collarbones that was kind of like nothing. We got to go to the movies a lot.

I have great admiration for the athlete, because I know what they go through. I know because Ray was fortunate to get a great horse and win the Breeders' Cup Turf, a two-million-dollar race.

My son was fourteen at the time, and he came to me one night and he says, "Mom, I have to go to Kentucky for the Breeders' Cup." And I said, "Son, it costs a lot of money just to go over there and back." He says, "I've got to go. Tell Dad." The next day Ray says, "Keary came up to me and he said, 'Dad, it'll mean so much to me; I have to go to this race.' " And Ray says, "We better let this kid go 'cause he's never asked me that way."

Okay, so we got our airline fares and everything. We missed one flight and then we're running to catch another flight and my luggage gets lost. Thank goodness my sister lives there 'cause I was in a panic when we got to the hotel. Sheila brought me about eight outfits.

That night Great Communicator's trainer, Thad Ackel, was talking to Ray and they're doing the strategy. I'm seeing people. And my son stayed in the hotel and bought a pizza 'cause he had met these other kids. Well, we get back to the room and Keary says, "Dad's gonna win the race tomorrow." I said, "Well, I sure hope so." He says, "No. Dad's gonna win the race. Do you know why? The great communicator is in town, Ronald Reagan, and they asked him who he would bet on and he said the Great Communicator." I like to flipped out. Reagan was on TV saying something like, "I don't go to horse racing, but I did see the lineup and if I'd have to bet on anybody, it would be the Great Communicator."

So the next morning it was like forty-four degrees, raining and cold all day, but I was never nervous the whole day. I had seen Juanita (Juanita Delahoussaye, wife of jockey Eddie Delahoussaye and a close friend) and all of them from California. And all that bunch of us was sitting around talking and Juanita says, "We're gonna go down in the racing office 'cause it's close to the winner's circle." I said, "Okay, fine. You know this place better than me." That was at Churchill.

So we're watching the race there. And Keary had been around all day long, but I hadn't seen him the last two races. I'd like to know where he is. So we're watching the race, and I could not believe it when Great Communicator and Ray are coming down the stretch. I was shouting, "He's coming back! He's coming back!"

And when the horse passed the finish line, all I could think of was where is Keary? With the security here, he won't be able to get through. My dad and I ran to the winner's circle, and I'm thinking, "I don't believe this. This kid wanted to be here so bad." Well, I turned around and see Keary. He had jumped a couple of balconies because the man wouldn't let him through. He got to the winner's circle. That was the greatest moment. I kept thinking, "God, if we'd told this kid 'no,' he would be at home watching this on national TV."

When Ray got off the horse and he came over to us with the orchids, and I was just...tears were coming down. And he handed one to me and kissed me. That was our greatest moment in horse racing, let me tell you. This is what it's all about.

Great Communicator paid $26.80. I went back home with $4,500 in my purse. I'll never forget that race. Ray did just a masterful ride. He just nursed this horse along. And then when they came around the turn to the eighth pole, they all came to him and he just took off.

We didn't sleep the whole night. And then when we got back home to California, the house was decorated in congratulations. That's what Ray remembers the most. You see, we lived on a street called Jockey Row. In between our house there was Gary Stevens on this side and then before him was Eddie Delahoussaye. And when we got back, our house was decorated like what we always did with the Kentucky Derby when Eddie won it. That was our best friend.

Ray said the next day when his first horse came out and the announcer Trevor Denman introduced him, he said people were congratulating him. He said the feeling...it just carries on. That's the meaning of what I'm telling you a horse can do.

We did have a low point in our life. We had opened a restaurant right across the street from Santa Anita racetrack August of 1989. It was called La Bon Vie. It means in French, "the good life." It was Cajun cooking. I had been to so many restaurants in California and around the country where they said "authentic Cajun." Well, I'd like to know where these authentic Cajun's are hiding because we never made gumbo with tomatoes! And my oldest sister was a chef, so we had the family involved: Two nieces, two nephews, two first cousins, and Ray and I. And my sister came from one of the best Cajun restaurants in Henderson, Louisiana, with recipes that you still can't find.

I knew in my heart we did it right because everything came from Louisiana, from the catfish to our bread. And we had it shipped there. So it was high expense and everything.

And Ray put out his heart and guts. Not to say his million and a half dollars. He'd come over and he'd chop onions or he'd peel our shrimp. I mean, he was there with my sister and us, and he was part of it, you know? It wasn't like, "Ray, give me your money. We're gonna make this restaurant..." It wasn't like that.

But we had to close it in 1991. We were devastated. The only thing I regret is having to close it and losing Ray's money. But I knew in my heart I put out the best food. And it came from where I said it came from. Not from down the street.

A lot of men that lost that much money and everything would just go, "I give it up from there." Ray came back stronger. And you see, I admire him for that more than anything. To overcome that was so tough.

When Ray's off, we spend time with the family. Oh I love it, going back home to Louisiana. It's like vacation for us — crawfish today, crabs tomorrow night — we get our fill of it! Ray's thing on off days is we go have lunch, and we go to a movie. He never was the type to golf all day or something like that. If we do it, it's something both of us are gonna do. It's him and me, you know.

CHAPTER 17

CHARLENE BURKHARDT

$\mathcal{T}$attoo Artist

$\mathbf{A}$s a pari-mutuel clerk at Chicago Thoroughbred tracks, Charlene Burkhardt for years was in the unique position of selling tickets on many horses that she had tattooed.

Burkhardt started as a racetrack groom in her late teens, then entered the ranks of the mutuel clerks in 1974 at Sportsman's Park in suburban Chicago. She was among the first female mutuel clerks. In 1986, she took on the additional role of official horse tattooer at the Chicago tracks for the Thoroughbred Racing Protective Bureau, the agency that keeps horses' tattoo numbers.

The tattoo, comprising one letter and five numbers, is applied to a horse's upper lip in a procedure that takes about fifteen minutes and involves quick insertions of dye-filled needles. It is an "invasive procedure, but not a painful one," said Burkhardt. A state-employed identifier then checks the tattoos each time a horse enters the paddock before a race. The numbers inside the horse's lip must correspond to those on his foal papers or the horse cannot compete.

Charlene Burkhardt was
one of the first female
pari-mutuel clerks.

Burkhardt estimates that she tattooed about 1,300 horses a year during the twelve years she performed the job. Tattoo artists who worked on former basketball star Dennis Rodman wouldn't even take out their needles for what she was paid: thirteen dollars per horse.

Among her favorite "clients," Burkhardt said, were Unbridled and Hansel, champion three-year-old colts of 1990 and '91, respectively, both of whom she "marked for life" at Arlington Park when they were two-year-olds. Burkhardt had favorite clients in her job as a mutuel clerk, too — but not as many by comparison. "Dealing with people is tougher than dealing with horses," she said.

Burkhardt worked both jobs until 1998 when she decided to leave the racetrack after twenty-five years to try another occupation. Since 1999 she has made her living as an over-the-road trucker.

A divorced mother of two grown children, Burkhardt is a resident of Caseyville, Illinois, where she lives in the house, built by her father, in which she grew up.

I was born in East St. Louis, Illinois, in 1950. My maiden name was Sumner. It's Irish. My dad died when I was five. He was a contractor. He built houses. He got killed in an accident on the job site — fell through a roof. So I don't know a lot about him. One thing I can tell you is that I still have all his tools. Had my dad lived, I would have definitely been a carpenter.

My mother was from a farming family down in southern Illinois. I had two brothers. My eldest brother died a month before

I was born. He was sixteen. Then five years later my father died. I don't know how my mother got through those things. My mom was emotionally out to lunch. I felt that. She just tried to get through the days.

My mom always let me have an animal when I was growing up. I think I transferred everything I had to them. I don't see dogs as dogs; I don't see horses as horses — I see them as beings.

I had a friend years ago who was trying to be a jockey. I asked him once if he ever thanked those horses for what they did. You see jockeys patting their mounts on the neck after races. He said, "No, I never do that. They're just horses." I knew right then he would never be a good jockey. And he wasn't. He works in the post office in New York City.

I used to tell my mom that I would give up anything, even my Barbie doll, if she'd let me have a horse. Giving up that doll was like the ultimate offering or sacrifice. We didn't have a big enough place, so I couldn't have one. But right across the street from us was a farm with horses, and I was there all — I mean all — of the time.

I had a girlfriend who dated a valet at Fairmount Park. She asked me to go to the races one time. When I got there, I was like, I've arrived! I belong here. The horses, the activity, the adrenaline I felt...I just felt like I belonged.

What I remember so intensely is the smell of the barns. To this day, if I could bottle it for perfume I would. I love that smell. I'd come home and tell that to my son and he'd go, "Oh, mom…" It's not good to most people. But it smells good to me. Am I wacko?

When I started working at the track, my mom about had a heart attack. She would say, "When are you going to get a real job?" I'd tell her, "Mom, this is my real job. This is the real deal." I was grooming horses at Fairmount. I was nineteen. I'd started to go to college, but I wasn't ready for it then. *(Editors' note: In 1990, Burkhardt earned an associate's degree in business management from Harper College in Palatine, Illinois.)*

One of the first trainers I worked for in Chicago was a real nice man, but he did most of his early morning training from a cot in his tack room. He was a married man. But he led what you could call an active social life without his wife. He used to lie on the cot in the mornings, hung over, suffering. He'd be moaning, "Booze and broads, booze and broads, they're killing me." One of us asked him once why he didn't give up this woman he was staying out all night with. He'd say, "I want to, but she's beautiful, I'm in loooove…" Then he'd moan and lie back down on the cot. It was hilarious.

I found a family at the racetrack. I think it's probably a dys-functional family, but they hang together. Right now I'm driving a truck. But I always feel like if I needed people to care for me, even if it was superficial — a place to live, or where I could borrow a few dollars — I could go back to the racetrack and make a living and survive there. Somebody will know you.

The people at the track mean a lot to me because of their connection with animals. Sure, I know there are people there who are better with them than others. But I know there are people there who would sooner starve than not have their horses eat.

I remember going into [trainer] Moises Yanez' barn and he had a sofa there and it was full of goats! He bought it for the goats to lay on. Now, who in the outside world would understand that?

I was twenty-one years old when I met my ex-husband...husband to be and ex-husband to be. I wasn't dating. I was happy just grooming horses. These girls I was working with said, "You've got to start going out with somebody." I said, "Nope, I'm happy the way I am." One day we were sitting outside the track kitchen at Oaklawn Park and Gary [Burkhardt] walks out the door. I said to this friend who was always after me about dating, "Oh, okay — him!" So she gets me a date. It's true. I know, my life is just one big comedy skit.

My ex-husband was an assistant trainer to a man who got into "a little" trouble by charging for horses that were supposedly being boarded on a farm in Arkansas, except they were actually dead. My ex-husband didn't know anything about this. We'd gone to Chicago to set up the stable. So my ex-husband's boss sends all his remaining horses to my husband and says, "I'm not coming."

The man who owned those horses, Crowdus Baker, was president of Sears Roebuck. We didn't have a feed tub, a shank, a saddle, nothing. But Mr. Baker said for my ex-husband to train his horses.

He loaned Gary the money to buy equipment and said he could pay him back month by month. Which we did. Of course, it was self-serving, since Mr. Baker had twenty-five horses sitting on a van with no trainer. Still, he took a chance on Gary, which was great of him.

I can tell you honestly, and I don't think anyone on the backside would dispute this, my ex-husband was as knowledgeable a horse trainer as anyone. But when Mr. Baker died, it all changed. We were young; we didn't realize the clout he carried. We didn't understand that Gary had been getting things because of Mr. Baker — stalls and so on. So, some people pulled the rug out from underneath us. I can remember Gary being on the phone, and they would give him stalls, and then they would later call him back and take those stalls away. Or they would move him out of a barn to a worse barn so somebody else could go into the first one.

Gary used to say, "What did I do?" You know, at the racetrack, some people will eat you up and spit you out if they can. When I say they are a dysfunctional family, I mean some people can be very brutal. I think that's what plunged Gary into drinking.

A lot of trainers, their self-worth is staked on how their horses are doing. If they don't have good horses, they feel like it's a direct reflection on them. Gary didn't have any good horses. He'd tell me, "I'm embarrassed to go up there and saddle these horses." One time when things were going bad, I told him, "Gary, why don't you give up being a head trainer? Why not just be an assistant trainer or gallop horses?" He wouldn't do it. He thought people would think he "couldn't cut it."

At one point, we went to marital counseling. I'm not going to put all our problems on Gary's back. He drank and I bitched. I began to feel like I was raising another child. When we went to counseling, that's when I learned I was an enabler. The counselor said, "As long as you keep working day and night to support the family, he'll keep drinking."

One day the counselor said to Gary, "You know you're an alcoholic, don't you?" My ex-husband got so angry he walked out the door and slammed it so hard he broke the frame. The counselor walked out with me, and he said, "Charlene, I know he's an alcoholic, and you know he's an alcoholic, but Gary doesn't know he's an alcoholic." We got divorced in 1980. It left a bad taste in my mouth. In spite of it all, Gary is a good person.

I gave up rubbing horses after I had my daughter. To me, rubbing horses is like having children. The horses were my children. So, it was then a case of either it's the horses or my daughter. Naturally, the answer was "it's her."

But I needed a job. I heard the mutuel clerks were going to go out on strike and they might be hiring replacements. This was in 1974. I walked to a phone booth near where we were living — we didn't have a phone — and called Mr. [Robert] Hart, who was the mutuels manager at Sportsman's Park. The mutuel clerks' jobs were all political jobs. I didn't know that. So I'm calling Mr. Hart and asking him if I can get a job application. He's kind of laughing, but he said, "All right, you come in."

I drive to Sportsman's with my mom and the baby — Amy's a year old — and leave them there in the car. Then I wait and wait. Bob Hart made me stand out there for hours. Finally, he granted me this interview. I felt like I was meeting with the Pope.

I go into his office and he asks me, "Who's your clout?" And I'm like, "I don't even know what the word means. I don't have any of it anyway. I just want a job."

He starts telling me that if I don't "know somebody," he can't hire me. Then he says to me at one point, "Well, doll," and I said, "Now just listen. My name isn't 'doll', it's Charlene." And he looks at me and says, "Do you want to start work tomorrow?"

You know what? He turned out to be the closest thing I've ever had to a father in my life. I love Mr. Hart. I got into the union through him. The starting salary was $32.50 a day, which was great. As a groom I made eighty-two dollars a week. So, the clerk's money is better. But you don't groom horses for money. And the clerk's job was harder.

When I first started, I was leaving my daughter with a babysitter. I had to be at the track by noon every day. They had a situation called "the bricks." If you weren't in the union yet and didn't have any seniority, they could pick to work anybody they wanted. It's like being a piece of meat. It's, "Okay, I'll take that one today." So you stand there on the bricks — the floor of the grandstand — and wait for the mutuels manager to decide who he's going to use that day. It's depending on his mood, his whim.

Most people go to work every day and have a job. Not mutuel clerks. They are hired on an as-needed basis. It's a daily question. Deciding how many clerks to hire, they'll look at estimated attendance, the weather, how many clerks they used last year on that date, the racing card itself. At Sportsman's Park they would factor in when the welfare checks came out. When the checks come, people come out and bet. It's kind of sick that I would know at the first of every month, when the welfare checks came out, that I'd get to work. Not many people go to work on that basis.

There would be maybe thirty of us on the bricks every day. Me and three or four others were the first women to start as clerks in Chicago. Women weren't allowed in the union before that. This was 1974. I think they saw the handwriting on the wall about minority rights and hiring; that's why they would hire us. One of the women was a black lady, Olivia Pittman, and I think management was afraid of lawsuits over discrimination. The Racing Board was also starting to put pressure on the tracks to hire minorities. So I got into the union riding on the coattails of a black woman.

I got into the union on December 2, 1975. Every mutuel clerk remembers exactly when he got in the union. Because once you're in, you're picked up on a seniority basis. So you remember your date and you know the seniority dates of every clerk around you. You look around, and if you see there are a lot of people there with less seniority, you know, "well, I've got a shot today."

There were many men clerks who were not happy seeing us

women there. They would say, "Why aren't you at home raising your kids?" I'd say, "If you want to pay me, I'll go home."

I could talk with them and walk the walk, but there were a lot of nights I went home and cried. Sometimes the men would be as vulgar as they could to try to intimidate us. To show us we "didn't belong." My mom was my best supporter. She'd say, "Go back. Just swallow it and go back." And I would. I pretended like it didn't matter. I had to take on a certain attitude, a toughness, that I didn't really like.

That first day Mr. Hart sent me to the two-dollar show window to work with a clerk named Frank. Do you know what touting is? Frank was touting all his customers. He tells one guy, "you bet on the [number] one horse," and then he gives another horse to the second guy, and the guy after that, and so on. So one of these bettors is going to have a winner and, supposedly, be grateful and come back and give Frank some money for sharing his "inside information." If a horse didn't run good and one of the guys he'd touted would come back to Frank to complain, Frank would say, "Oh, he had a sore forelock." Or, "the damned jock dropped the whip." Frank would never have even seen the race!

Frank used to give Christmas cards to his regular customers during December when they would come to his window. He had no "inside information" whatsoever, but these people thought he did. So I'm looking over his shoulder that first day on the job, being trained, and I'm wondering, "What are you doing?"

But Frank also taught me how to do the real job. I wasn't interested in learning how to tout people. This was before the computer terminals, working the two-dollar show window. After a while, Mr. Hart moved me to a ten-dollar window. He said, "Be careful."

Because you are responsible for any mistakes you make with the money. If you don't balance at the end of the day, if you come up short — have less money than the machine shows you should have for the number of tickets you sold — then you have to make up the difference.

If you're over, it's yours. You get to keep it. But I would say for every one time you're over, it'll be one hundred times you're short. The worst hit — mistake — I took was $782. How did it happen? I had a brain cramp for about thirty seconds. This guy comes up to cash and then bet. Instead of punching in one-dollar trifecta boxes like he wanted, I put ten-dollar trifecta boxes in. He had money coming, but I paid him on the basis of deducting the cost of the one-dollar tri boxes, not the ten-dollar ones that I mistakenly punched. At the end of the day, I push the button that says how much money is going to be in my cash box. I look down there and I know it's not even close. I had to come up with the $782.

You've got to stay alert. The biggest enemy a mutuel clerk has is down time. When you're busy, you're hitting it, you're on top of it. And you have to understand gamblers. They're not like Betty and Mary that come on the weekend and bring twenty dollars with them. The gamblers, they eat and breathe this; it's in their blood. Before the horses get to the paddock, they're not going to bet a dime. They want to look at the horses, watch them. If they can, they like to see them go into the gate. They'd probably like to see them come out, too, before they bet.

We'll have guys standing at the window at post time saying "two-hundred dollars to win on the five...No, no, he's not going into the gate right, no." And there are customers who want to cheat you, want to run roughshod over you, try to rush you into punching in a bet. Then if the horse loses they'll try to come back and say you gave them the wrong ticket. So you've got to be careful. You say, "Okay, pal, you want this ticket or not? Is it or isn't it?"

But you meet a lot of nice people, too. I had a lady customer who was born in Holland. She went there on vacation one time and brought me back a beautiful porcelain shoe. There was a guy who was a retired fireman. He would bring us baskets of fruit. It meant they thought of you as a person. I think some people come to the racetrack because they're lonely.

I had a black guy as a customer for years. He was a deaf mute. He would write out his bets on a slip and hand it to me. People used to be mean to him. The ones behind him would start hollering at him. That's the one time I would get mad. I would tell them, "He's got as much right to be here as anybody. Drop dead. If you don't like it, I can see fifty other windows. Go find one."

One day in 1986, my friend Mary Erickson (horse identifier for the Illinois Racing Board) came to me and said, "Charlene, would you be interested in coming back with the horses?" I said, "I don't think I could go back to being a groom — not with my kids and those hours and being a clerk." Mary said, "No, I don't mean grooming. I mean tattooing horses." I was like, "I never in my wildest dreams thought about that." She said, "Well, think about it."

I decided to do it. A lot of horsemen had their doubts that I could do the job well. I'm no big six-foot cowboy (she is five-foot-seven). But tattooing horses isn't a matter of strength. Horses respond best to finesse. Women work very well with horses. I don't know, maybe horses somehow respond to the nurturing instincts of women.

There is one tattooer at each racetrack. When the trainer pays the horsemen's bookkeeper for the tattooing, that generates a receipt. They put those receipts in an envelope. I would go and pick up the envelope every afternoon after the races. Then I would schedule the horses to be worked on the next morning. Much of this is done on a rush-job basis. A lot of people put off getting their horses tattooed. [As a result] I've tattooed horses at midnight, I've tattooed them on horse vans...there have been a lot of "emergencies."

I've been run out of places. One trainer ran me out of his barn. He had a gray filly that did not match her foal papers in any way, shape, or form. This guy was throwing stuff around the shed row and yelling at me to tattoo her. I told him I couldn't. I went to my car. He came out, still screaming at me and pounding on the hood of the car. He said something like, "You're nothing but a lowly tattooer. I don't need you." I just looked at him and said, "Yes, you do." And I drove off.

He went to the racing secretary's office in a rage and was throwing condition books around. Then he went to the stewards. But the ball was in my court. He had no serve. They couldn't help him because he had foal papers that didn't match the horse.

A few days later I was selling mutuel tickets in the track kitchen and he came in. I thought, "Uh, oh, here we go, right in front of people, him yelling at me again." But he walked right up to me and said, real nice and calm, "I need you." I said, "Good." And since he finally had gotten the correct foal papers, I could tattoo his filly. So I did.

Horses I tattooed were mainly between the ages of two and five. Most of them are two. This takes place at each horse's barn usually, but sometimes on a farm. The cost was fifty dollars a horse when I was last doing it. I did between thirteen and fifteen horses a day. You certainly couldn't make a living doing this. It's a part-time job. I got thirteen of the fifty dollars — and all the aggravation I could handle. If you're a horse, are you going to like the idea of somebody coming up to you and sticking a needle in your lip?

You have to take time with each horse. It's almost like taking your little kid to get a vaccination. Sometimes you can talk a horse into being brave when they don't want to be. Other times, they're not listening; they just want to kill you. You get a tranquilizer for the bad ones. But tranquilizing can work against you, too. In some cases, instead of slowing them down it makes them ten times more aggressive. Then you're in trouble.

Some horses you can talk to and touch and get them to embolden themselves, like they're feeling, "I can do this for you." They speak with their body language. Their ears and eyes tell you volumes about what they are capable of handling. The easiest to deal with are the young horses. By the time they get to be four or five, they know the tricks.

You use a five-inch handle on dye-filled needles you insert into their lips. It involves quick insertions into the lip with needles that are filled with vegetable dye. You put the needles in with physical force and impress them. It's not like an electric needle for other tattoos.

Either the trainer or a groom helps by holding the horses. You use a twitch to roll up the lip and expose it. That cuts off the circulation and makes the lip numb, like when you have a rubber band around your finger. It helps the horse by cutting off the pain. You don't want to hurt the horse. The twitch doesn't hurt them. They are living, breathing, feeling beings. Some are more caring than others — just like with people.

My nightmare horse was a filly that [owner-trainer-breeder] Frank Kirby had called Serene Sue. There was nothing serene about her when I was trying to tattoo her. She was aggressive; she was furious. I think she wanted to kill me. It was a terrible experience for both of us.

When this was going on, we had a real long shank on Serene Sue, and she threw a fit. She reared up, and the shank got wrapped around my leg. She ran out of the stall. It was the most frightening thing that ever happened to me. If she would have kept running, she would have dragged me with her. But when she got to the end of the shank, she stopped for just a split second and the groom had enough sense to reach up and grab her. The groom didn't unbuckle the halter; he just pulled it forward over her ears and off her head. Then she just went running on out of there. The groom probably saved my life.

I remember going home that night and lying in bed and replaying the whole scene. I wonder if jockeys do that after they've been thrown, have those replays.

Serene Sue went on to have babies and they were just as bad as she was. She was horrible. Her whole family was. They were there to make your life miserable, and they took relish in it.

I quit tattooing in 1998. Actually, I stopped both tattooing and being a mutuel clerk that same year. I'd been clerking almost twenty-five years. I wasn't having any fun anymore.

I'm talking more about the clerking than the tattooing. Dealing with people is harder than dealing with horses. Any time people have something with money riding on it, like horse-race betting, there's a chance for confusion and complaints. But I knew if I was going to leave the track, I'd have to cut the cord and quit both jobs. You've heard about how horses get sour? That's me, I guess. I got sour.

My son-in-law talked to me about driving trucks. He used to do it. I told him, "I just need some freedom — freedom from having a boss on my hands." So I went to school to learn how to do this, took a course at a junior college. I drive for the Covenant Company. They're based in Chattanooga. They have about five-thousand trucks on the road. It is amazing to me some of the people who drive trucks. There are two people driving for Covenant that have Ph.Ds. And then there are some people, just like at the racetrack (laughs), that maybe you wouldn't want to know.

I'll pick up my load in Markham, Illinois (south of Chicago), and usually go to Los Angeles and back, sometimes Atlanta. One day I'll have $4.5 million worth of computers in the back of that truck, the next day crates of cereal. When you have what they call a high-security load, like computers — these sometimes get hijacked — you never leave the truck unattended. I work with a guy named Bill McMaster, very nice guy. We're told if hijackers ever come up to the truck with a gun, give them the keys.

Would I ever go back to the racetrack? Not to the mutuels, but to the horses, yes. If I ever have enough money some day...well, my daughter and I both said we would buy a young horse and break him and bring him to the track.

Years ago when I worked as a groom, I used to rub a little horse called Doughnut Tree. He knew me, and I loved him. If I could have picked him up in my arms and carried him, I would have. When I'd come into the barn in the mornings, he'd hear my voice and run to the door of the stall and nicker.

In fact, today I keep his wolf tooth in my sewing box. So you can see — the connection to horses is still there for me.

ACKNOWLEDGMENTS

In addition to the interview subjects, our thanks go to these people who helped make this book possible: *John Brokopp, Joaquin Cambray, the staff of Eclipse Press, Andy Hansen, Bobby Kelly, Bob Kieckhefer, Frier C. McCollister, Jim Miller,* and *Dave Zenner.*

JOHN MCEVOY, a graduate of the University of Wisconsin, is a former newspaper reporter and college English teacher who subsequently served as Midwest editor, then senior writer for *Daily Racing Form*. He is the author of *Great Horse Racing Mysteries — True Tales From The Track*, published by Eclipse Press in 2000. McEvoy also is the author of the 1995 book *Through the Pages of Daily Racing Form*, an  historical overview of American Thoroughbred racing based on material that had appeared in that newspaper's first one hundred years. He has published a book of poetry and his *Stiffereeno*, a crime novel with a horse racing theme, will be published in 2002. He and his wife, Judy, live in Evanston, Illinois; they have three children and three grandchildren.

JULIA MCEVOY is an independent writer and producer whose work can be heard on National Public Radio. In her fourteen years in radio, McEvoy has produced award-winning documentaries and won the 1991 Eclipse Award for Best Radio Coverage of Thoroughbred Racing. Her stories have aired on NPR's *All Things Considered* and  *Morning Edition,* as well as *Marketplace* and *Latino USA*.

McEvoy studied journalism at the University of Wisconsin-Madison and the Centre des Etudes de la Science et la Techniques de l'Information in Dakar, Senegal. Formerly, McEvoy was director of television at Arlington Park and a publicist at Gulfstream Park racetrack in Florida. She lives with her husband, Christopher, and their family in Evanston, Illinois.

Linda Rice .... Barbara D. Livingston

Patti Browne and Donna Barton Brothers ....Tina Hines,
Keeneland, Bill Denver

Charlsie Cantey .... Lydia Williams, Anne M. Eberhardt

Jenine Sahadi .... Katey Barrett, Gretchen Henney Sheridan

Alice Chandler .... Anne M. Eberhardt, Delaware Park

Francesca (Maria) Rabadan .... Joseph Oliver

Barbara D. Livingston .... Nancy Thorkildsen,
courtesy of Barbara D. Livingston

Mary Scollay .... courtesy of Mary Scollay

Christine Janks .... Bowerman-Camelback Inn, Four Footed Fotos

Jane Goldstein .... Benoit & Associates, courtesy of Jane Goldstein

Christine Salvino .... Four Footed Fotos

Donna Porter .... Four Footed Fotos

Sheryl Stefanowicz .... Four Footed Fotos

Zoe Cadman .... Four Footed Fotos, Joseph Oliver

Maryjean Wall .... Tom Hall, Charles Bertram

Dot Sibille .... Four Footed Fotos

Charlene Burkhardt .... courtesy of Charlene Burkhardt

Cover and back photos ....Barbara D. Livingston